Walking through the History of
Bishop's Cleeve

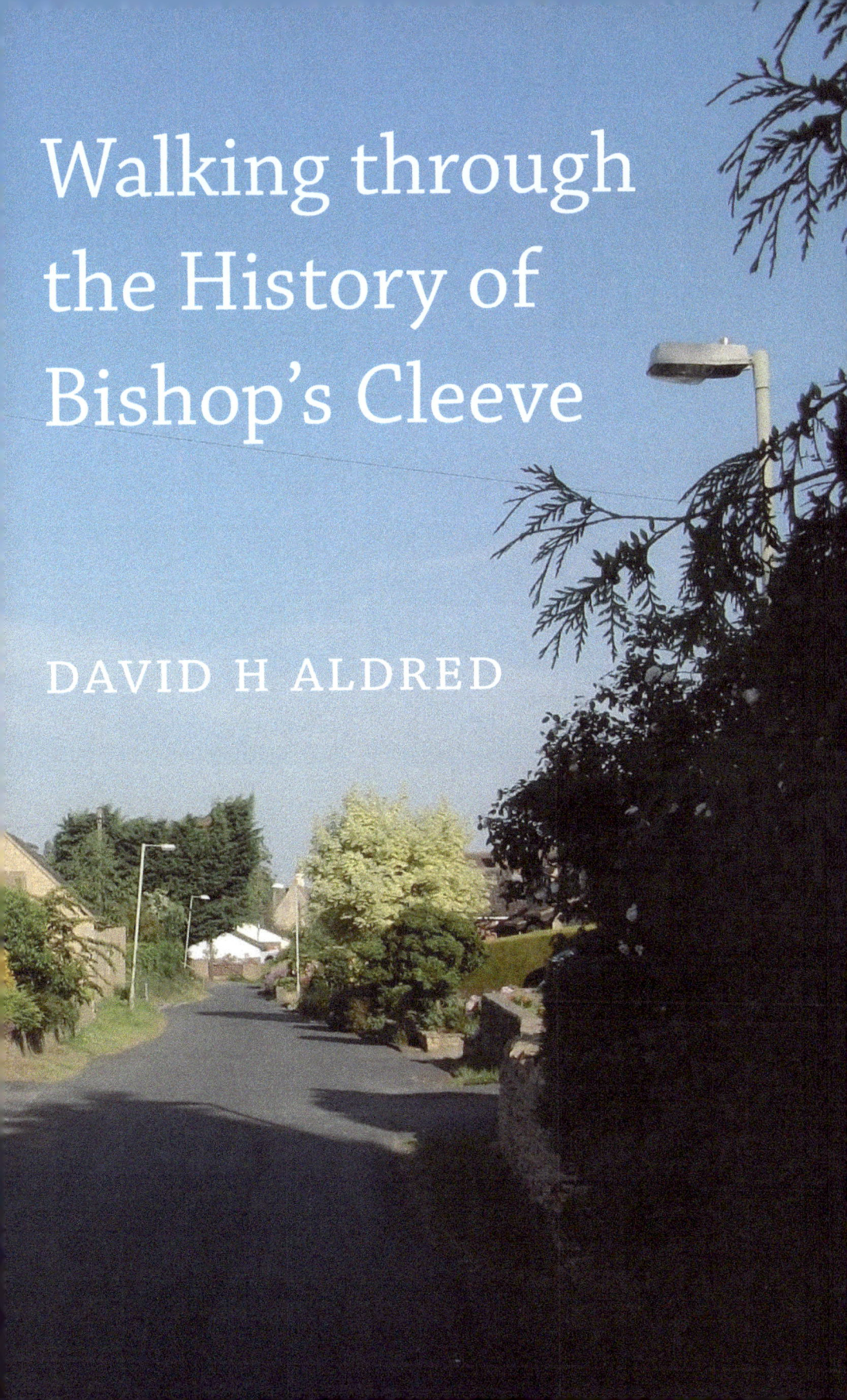

First published in the United Kingdom in 2022
by The Hobnob Press,
8 Lock Warehouse, Severn Road, Gloucester GL1 2GA
www.hobnobpress.co.uk

© David Aldred, text and images, 2022

The Author hereby asserts his moral rights to be identified as the Author of the Work.

All rights reserved. No part of this publication may be reproduced, stored in a retrieval system, or transmitted in any form or by any means, electronic, mechanical, photocopying, recording or otherwise, without the prior permission of the publisher and copyright holder.

British Library Cataloguing in Publication Data
A catalogue record for this book is available from the British Library

ISBN 978-1-914407-44-4

Typeset in Chaparral Pro, 11/14 pt
Typesetting and origination by John Chandler

CONTENTS

Preface	7
Introduction: Before you go	9
Walk around the centre of the village	17
Extended walk along Station Road and Priory Lane	55
A Tour around Saint Michael and All Angels Church	68
Case Study 1: Oldacre's	78
Case Study 2: Cleeve Hall	83
Case Study 3: Cleeveway Manor	92
Case Study 4: The Priory	99
Case Study 5: The Old Manor House	111
Case Study 6: Eversfield House	114
Glossary	117
Further reading	119

PREFACE

It is now twelve years since my most recent book on the history of Bishop's Cleeve appeared. In that time there have been two main developments. Firstly, the population of the village has increased by over one third and secondly that expansion has allowed archaeologists to find out more about past landscapes in and around the village. So it seems appropriate at this time to write another book on the village's rich history, but from a different point of view, through three walks around the historic centre. The main part of the book comprises the walks and these are followed by six case studies of sites of particular significance. The text incorporates photographs of the village which I have used before but many are published here for the first time. I hope that those which have been seen before are put into a greater context than when they were previously published. In order to enable a greater understanding of key historical words and a wider knowledge of the village's history, I have added a glossary and a further reading list at the end of the case studies.

I have many people to thank for their assistance in different ways. Geoff Newsum of Gotherington gave me the idea of using a walk as the means for communicating my knowledge of the history of Bishop's Cleeve. Professor Christopher Dyer and Dr Steven Bassett have helped with the medieval period and I benefited from the late Eunice Powell's knowledge of St Michael's Church and have used some of her illustrations. Rachel Hassell, Sherborne School's archivist, provided details on the two Eagar brothers who died in the Great War. I have learnt much about the recent history of the village from John Burton, Pam Crook, Mike Edwards, Caroline Meller, Margaret Minett, Susanna Webb and Susanne Weir. I am grateful to the owners of the properties in my case studies: Sally and Adam Butcher, the Hancox family, the Dessalles family, Stephen and Susan Shepherd and Vistry Cotswold. I hope you enjoy reading the case studies, but please respect the owners' privacy. I have used photographs from my own collection, including those taken by myself, and I have also relied on the collections of the late Bill Potter, Tim Curr and Mike Ralls. Bill took his own photographs but

Tim and Mike copied those lent from other people. I have endeavoured to trace the origins of these photographs but it has not always been possible to link the correct name to every photograph and so I trust that a list of names will be acceptable to the donors. I apologise for any names which I have left out and will correct this in any future publication: Derrick Blake, David Denley, Ann Everson, Jim Gardner, Doreen Jenkins, Margaret Minett, Nancy Minett, Molly Quilter, Mike Smith, Grace Staite, Jim Stevenson, Susanna Webb and Susanne Weir. I am aware that some are no longer with us. My thanks go also to the staff at Bishop's Cleeve library, Gloucestershire Archives and Cheltenham Local Studies for their unfailing assistance and help. Where specific acknowledgement has been required I have indicated this in the captions. I have deposited Bill Potter's and Tim Curr's collections in the Gloucestershire Archives. Finally I must thank John Chandler of Hobnob Press for his support in the publishing of the book and my wife Margaret for her forbearance and encouragement during my researching and writing and also for commenting upon my first drafts. Any errors remain mine alone.

David Aldred
November 2022

INTRODUCTION
BEFORE YOU GO

PEOPLE HAVE BEEN LIVING in and around the centre of Bishop's Cleeve for a very long time. When Tesco was being built in 1998 archaeologists from Wessex Archaeology concluded people had been living continuously on and around that site since the Early Bronze Age (c.2000 BC-c.1500 BC). Although isolated finds of flint from the Mesolithic, or Middle Stone Age. (c.10,000 BC–c.4000 BC) and the Neolithic, or New Stone Age, (c.4000 BC-c.2000 BC) indicate that people had been in the Bishop's Cleeve area in earlier times, little evidence of settlements has been found. In 2020 archaeologists working on the former Nortenham allotments at the north end of the bypass did find pottery, as well as flint, dated to the Early Neolithic period (c.4000 BC) which suggested a short-lived settlement; people at that time moved around in the landscape. At the time of writing this is the earliest known settlement site in the vicinity of the historic village centre.

An area stretching from Tesco to Cleeve Hall, Lidl, Gilders Paddock and Maxwell Place was extensively excavated at the end of the last century. Pottery, animal bones, ditches and signs of buildings dating from the Bronze Age (c.2000 BC-c.800 BC) to the 8th century AD were discovered, strongly suggesting that people had lived without a break in this area but not on exactly the same site. There was evidence of farmsteads and fields and tantalising evidence of a Romano-British villa (dated from pottery to 2nd-4th century AD) perhaps near or under Cleeve Hall, which is still awaiting discovery. There was no village in these years, just dispersed farmsteads. Archaeologists discovered five farmsteads dating from c.400 BC to 4th century AD during the building of the bypass in the late 1970s and early 1980s. More recent excavations between November 2014 and December 2016 on the Cleevelands estate to the west of the Evesham Road and in 2015 at Homelands Farm between Evesham Road and Gotherington Lane discovered two Middle Bronze Age (c.1500 BC-c.1100 BC) settlements. None of these sites was

Excavations by Birmingham University on the Dean's Lea/Greenacre Way site discovered an Iron Age farmstead, typical of those found in the area (Birmingham University)

known before the modern expansion of the village.

The first evidence of a village comes indirectly from a document dated 777–779 AD in which King Offa of Mercia granted land to a *monasterium* at St Michael and All Angels *aet Clife*. There are no more details about the settlement but we can make some inferences from the grant. A *monasterium* was a community of priests who would take Christianity to the surrounding area. The use of the word *monasterium* has led to a persistent myth that Bishop's Cleeve once had a medieval monastery with monks, as at Gloucester Cathedral or Tewkesbury Abbey; this was never the case. It is feasible that people had moved and did move to supply the needs of this small community of priests, moving from their dispersed settlements to create a small settlement around the *monasterium*. At its centre stood the church in its own grounds, or precinct, which is still recognisable today, bounded by Church Road, Cheltenham Road, Station Road and School Road; the heart of the old village. Within a century of the grant most of the land came into the hands of the Bishop of Worcester where it remained until 1561. The addition of 'Bishop's' was first recorded in 1284 to distinguish it from Cleeve Prior north of Evesham, which was held by the Prior of Worcester. A small portion was not granted to the bishop but to a priest, who was recorded in the Domesday Book of 1087. Throughout the Later Middle Ages (1086-c.1550) there were two manors in the village and these will be discovered on the walk.

Domesday Book gives a first view of the settlement, although it has to be interpreted with care. The land was divided between the bishop and the priest, who both rented most of it out and kept a demesne for themselves. The land rented to the villagers provided enough work for sixteen ploughs, the bishop's demesne had work for three ploughs and the rector's two ploughs. Historians have estimated that a team of up to eight oxen, depending on the nature of the soil, could plough about 100a (42ha) each and so these figures give us an idea of the extent of the arable land. At that time half of that land would have been planted each year and the other half left fallow, or unploughed, so livestock could graze on it and manure it. The entry then tells us sixteen villagers, nineteen smallholders and eight slaves lived in the settlement; the latter would have worked for the bishop. We know they were given their freedom shortly after 1087. Finally, Bushcombe (i.e. bishop's valley) Wood was also recorded and was possibly larger than it extends today.

How many people lived in the village at different times in the past is difficult to discover because before the first census of 1801 all figures are estimates. The first four figures below represent families, the first from Domesday Book and then the combined recorded totals from the bishop's and rector's manors. To emphasise that these figures need to be viewed with caution, we know that in 1299 some of these recorded tenants had sublet to unrecorded subtenants.

1087	1299	1349	1546
45	98	70	52

These later figures are based on individuals, firstly on church figures and then the census. The last figure is an estimate:

1551	1676	1775	1801	1851	1931	1951	2022
203	275	438	476	740	641	4547	18000

Numbers before 1801 might be approximations but some trends are clear: the increase until 1299, which led to the village expanding in three directions – Abovetown, Southtown and Newtown (more details on the walks); the impact of the Black Death of 1348–49 and shrinkage of those three areas; the slow increase in the size of the farming community till 1851; stagnation and slow decline until 1931 as agriculture could no longer sustain the population; the impact of Smiths Industries in 1951 and the continuing modern population growth since the 1980s.

The workings of the bishop's manor dominated the village during the Later Middle Ages but with the religious changes of the Reformation, it eventually came into the hands of Queen Elizabeth I in 1601. Three years later she sold it to two wealthy Londoner merchants Peter Vanlore and William Blake. From that time onwards the land and buildings were sold off in bits and pieces until by the time of the passing of the Enclosure Act in 1838 (see below) there were 148 registered landowners in the parish, although this also included Southam and part of Gotherington which had never been part of the bishop's manor. They ranged from large landowners such as John Morris of The Priory with over 70a (30ha) to Ann Spencer who owned and lived on a one acre (½ha) plot in Priory Lane, which you will see on your walk. Many of the owners lived away from the village and rented out their farms, farmland and houses, which led to a mobile population as many tenants moved in and out quite frequently. Conversely the rector's manor remained largely intact with its tenants paying their rent to the church, although its extent slowly shrunk over time and it became known as glebe land, so that its last remnant was the Nortenham allotment site of 10a (4ha) to the north of the village

The former allotments at the northern end of the bypass were the last vestige of the glebe in 2022. The earliest reference to this land being part of the glebe was in 1389.

along the Evesham Road. The allotments were managed by the parish council but were handed back to the diocese in late 2019 for a housing development after new allotments had been created behind them at the Cleevelands development. Until well into the twentieth century renting rather than owning a house was the norm. In a survey of 1911 of the 77 houses, farms and cottages in and around the centre of the village, only 20 were owner-occupied, with thirteen belonging to men and seven belonging to women. This has provided difficulties for researching the history as tenants moved much more often than owner-occupiers.

The biggest change to the village before the arrival of Smiths Industries was the enclosure of the open fields which began in 1838 and took nine years to complete. One of the reasons for the delay was that many of the 148 landowners argued their case to continue to use Cleeve Common to pasture their animals. By the process of enclosure the remaining open field strips were swept away and a modern landscape of individual fields was created; fields which over the next century and a half were increasingly sold off for housing and other developments which have led to the large village we know today. The effects on the landscape can be appreciated by comparing an 1813 estate map with the 1847 Enclosure Map. The 1813 map shows all the land belonging to what became Cleevelands Farm. Large areas are blank because they were not owned by the farm, but the pattern of scattered strips is clear to see. Compare that with the same area in the 1847 map, with its regularly shaped fields created on paper by the enclosure commissioners using pencil and ruler. The whole process cost £1226 (approximately £157,000 today) and each landowner paid relative to the area of land allocated to him or her. So ended nearly a thousand years of communal farming and landowners were now largely free to exploit their land unhindered by centuries' old by-laws, customs and practices. Under favourable weather conditions surviving relics of the corrugated ridge and furrow landscape of the open fields can still be discerned looking west along the bypass.

Enclosure occurred much later in Bishop's Cleeve than many of the surrounding villages and it came at a time when English villages dependent upon agriculture began to lose population as increasing mechanisation and changing farming practices reduced employment and people began to move away to towns and cities which they thought offered better life prospects than the unrelenting demands of the

An estate map of 1813 (Gloucestershire Archives D5474/1)

Part of the 1847 enclosure map showing the same area (Gloucestershire Archives Q/RI/45)

agricultural year. Like many such villages it entered a period of decline and decay. Orchards and market gardens developed as a reaction to this general decline in agriculture but could not replace the jobs which had been left. It was the arrival of Smiths Industries which led to the creation of the modern village. 300 acres (125 ha) of land at Kayte Farm, near The Newlands, were bought in April 1939 as war loomed and the London factory on the North Circular Road was considered a possible war target. The Grange, now best seen from the bypass, was also purchased and the first sign of the coming factory was a large number of caravans placed in its grounds to accommodate key workers. The first factory building was opened in May 1940. Houses followed, Meadoway between the village and the factory in 1941 and then the large estate to the south of the village along Tobyfield Road. Here was a catalyst for the future expansion of the village; Cleeveview

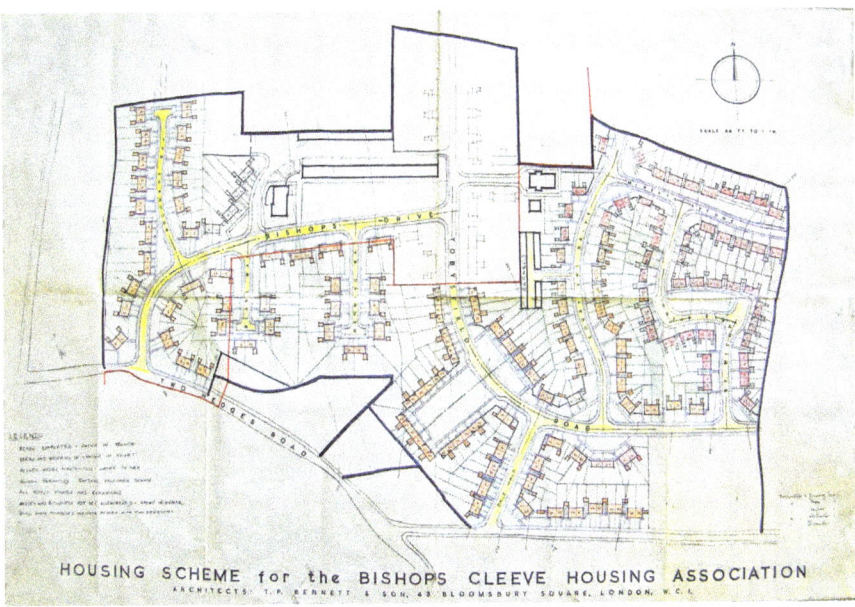

Plan of 1951 showing the first stages of Smiths' estate (Gloucestershire Archives DA21/711).

estate in the 1960s, Crown Drive estate in the 1970s and then the massive expansion on completion of the bypass since the 1980s of the Homelands and Cleevelands estates, plus houses along the road to Stoke Orchard. Infilling and redevelopment have also taken place in the historic parts of the village but much of its story can still be discerned in the buildings and scenes which survive. I hope these walks help you to understand better its rich history

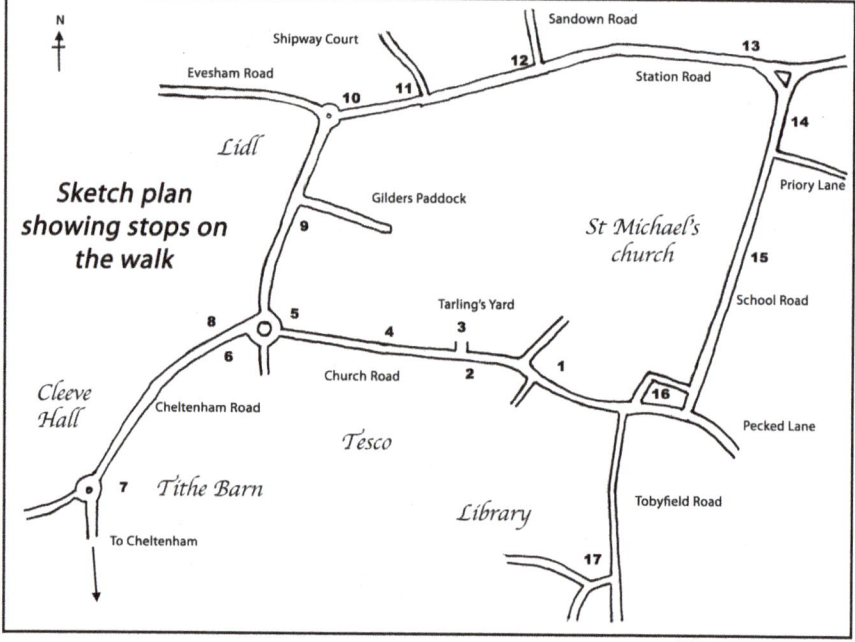

right: The central area of the village from the 1883 25-inch Ordnance Survey map (National Library of Scotland)

WALK AROUND THE CENTRE OF THE VILLAGE

THIS WALK through the history of the historic centre of Bishop's Cleeve starts outside the Post Office (Stop 1). Here you are standing on one of the oldest features of the village, a pre-historic routeway which dates back to at least the Iron Age (c.800BC to 43AD). The route starts from the A38 south of Tewkesbury through Stoke Orchard, continuing as Stoke Road to Bishop's Cleeve and then eastwards along Pecked Lane, although the line past the war memorial is relatively recent (see below), and then it follows the footpath to Woodmancote before following Stockwell Lane to reach a small Iron Age settlement by the stables on Cleeve Common before joining other long distance routes across the common.

Church Road looking west

Turn left and compare the view with this photograph taken in the early years of the last century. The Royal Oak suffered a serious roof fire about fifty years ago but enough roof timbers remained to indicate the eastern part which stands on a low stone wall had originally been cruck-built. Crucks are the large curved timbers which take the weight of the roof, as shown in the sketch. You will see more buildings with crucks as you walk round. They probably date to the 1400s, if not earlier. Obviously the buildings have been changed during the intervening centuries but they remain the oldest inhabited buildings in the village. The Royal Oak was recorded as two houses in 1839 with a barn, yard and stable behind and so was then probably operating as a farm. The Ordnance Survey map of 1883 marks it as a beer house and we

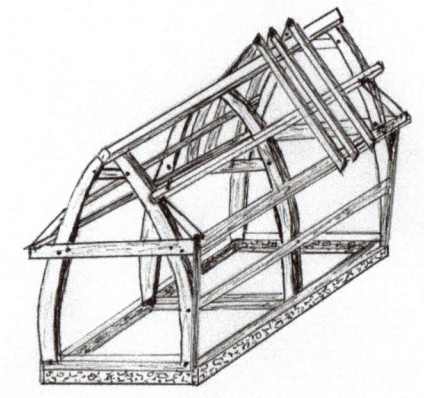

Simplified sketch showing cruck construction

Centre of the village from the 1839 Tithe map (Gloucestershire Archives GDR/TI/26)

know that in 1915 it was owned by Showells Brewery in Birmingham and occupied by Mrs Emily Tarling. During the Second World War the village's Pig Club held its AGM there. In 1946 the secretary noted that ninety pigs had been sent for slaughter in the last year of the war, which had ended the previous August.

Now notice how the two early 19th-century cottages on the right have been demolished to allow the entrance into the car park; the exposed timbers of the Royal Oak which you can see are those of an interior wall. In 1885 the nearer of the two demolished cottages was recorded as the post office. It was again serving as the post office in the 1920s. Looking towards Cleeve Hill, Aston Court stands where Egremont Villa, a rather pretentious early 19th-century farmhouse with a barn stood until 1991. Part of Church Road was straightened here in 1966 when the cruck-built timber-framed house to the left of Egremont Villa was demolished. In the Later Middle Ages (1066 to *c.*1550) this area of the village was called Cheapside ('cheap' is linked to 'chipping' which means 'market') and the thatched house became one of the last surviving houses linking back directly to that time. On your left the garden with its retaining Cotswold stone wall was replaced by the existing shops in 1961 as Church Road developed into the village's main commercial centre. Cheapside was part of the rector's manor and in 1396-97 the rector paid 4s.6d. (22½p) for four shops to be re-roofed. The gardens are evidence that the medieval buildings had been mostly demolished even before the 1839 Tithe map was drawn, but that map records that Robert Sollis still operated his blacksmith's shop where the war memorial now stands. It seems historically fitting that shops once again trade in this part of the village.

In the 1890s William Gilder was landlord of the Old Elm Tree Inn, which we know was in existence in 1728 as a small house, if not yet a beer house. It was replaced over a century ago by the large brick and stone building opposite you at the entrance to the car park. By 1959 the pub had closed as the building was bought by the county council which re-opened it the next year as the village's youth club. Since then it has experienced a number of different uses but the name is still in use to remind villagers of its earlier existence. Until 1984 the adjoining

The Old Elm Tree

property was the home of Beckingsale's grocer's shop 'Grocery provisions with a personal service'. Arthur Beckingsale came here in 1907 to open his shop with the village post office. It became famous for the quality of its produce and personal service. After Arthur died in 1940 it was taken over by Norman Blake who was joined later by his son Derrick. When they closed the door for the last time in 1984 a village institution

Norman and Derrick Blake in Beckingsale's shop just before closure

disappeared. From these large early 20th-century brick buildings move on to the restored timber-framed building next door; one of the village's most interesting buildings (Stop 2).

Known historically as Laburnum Cottage, its origins lay in another cruck-built house which dates to the 1400s. In 1445 the village is said to have suffered a disastrous fire and some of the surviving medieval buildings could be the new houses which were built after this event. We know this because the villagers appealed to parliament to be relieved of paying taxes, but we are not sure about the details. It could be that the claim was just a plea to parliament to avoid paying taxes and because it is not mentioned in any other record, we are not sure how widespread was

When Laburnum Cottage was renovated in 2007, this section of wattle and daub was uncovered. The wattles probably came from Bushcombe Wood. All the Medieval timber-framed buildings you will pass would originally have had this between the timbers before being replaced much later by bricks.

the fire or whether it ever occurred. It's possible some buildings survive from an earlier date. In the Later Middle Ages Laburnum Cottage was probably the home of a farmer of half a yardland (i.e. 12a [5ha]), eight of whom were recorded in the village in 1299 and they seem to have lived in this part of the village. Twelve acres was not enough to support a family as half that land lay fallow each year and so the farmer had also to work for wages for wealthier farmers or develop a craft. Even with any sons working, the income brought in by farmers' wives and daughters selling fruit, eggs, butter and cheese in the village or in Cheltenham and Winchcombe markets, would have been essential for survival.

Now look down the road and compare the view with that of c.1900. The villager carrying buckets on a yoke has obviously gone, but

Church Road c.1900

the timber-framed building (29 Church Road) is another which probably housed the family of a half-yardlander and dates back to the late 1400s. This was built around a box frame which was a more sophisticated method of building because the walls carried the weight of the roof rather than the crucks. However, it was also built with the main room, the hall, open to the roof and the roof timbers still carry the soot from the open fire in the hall. Smoke made its way out of the house as best it could. When a ceiling above the hall and the necessary chimney were installed *c.*1550, a mummified cat was placed under the rafters to ward off evil spirits and witches. Obviously the western end of the house was rebuilt in brick in the early 20th century. Next stands Greyholme. The drip moulds above the windows were fashionable in the late 17th or early 18th century at a time when it was most unusual for small houses in the village to be built of Cleeve Hill stone. It seems never to have served as a farmhouse. Look out for other houses with drip mould features as you walk round the village.

Opposite Laburnum Cottage turn into Tarling's Yard (Stop 3). William Tarling was the wheelwright here in 1889 where a carpenter and blacksmith were also recorded. Don't miss the wheelwright's furnace immediately on your left as you go in. This was built in 1907 for heating the iron rims which were then shrunk on to wooden wheels. The historic use of the yard as a hive of activity for craftsmen is reflected today in its small commercial units. Look for the two date stones which tell you when it was built. Originally this was

The Tarling family c.1890

Tarling's Yard in 1979

the farmyard of 29 Church Road and the clue is the 'L' shape of the house which incorporates its former barn. Internally a small gap still existed between the two buildings, which was partly filled by a re-used

Church Road in 1977 before the building of Mill Parade. In the distance the old barn can be seen with the semi-detached houses behind it and the Spinning Wheel in front

cruck taken from a lost building. The end facing you of the former barn provides an excellent example of a box-framed building. As you leave Tarling's Yard notice how the parish office opposite looks like a barn, built deliberately to reflect the appearance of the last barn to survive along Church Road, demolished to make way for the parish office in 2009. Although it was probably built in the 18th century, the archaeologists found evidence of an earlier barn from either the Romano-British or the medieval period. They weren't sure. The small park created to commemorate the millenium lies in what was the front gardens of a pair of mid-20th century semi-detached houses; the remainder of their gardens is now the car park. The single-storeyed white building on the edge of the photograph was known as the Spinning Wheel, having sold haberdashery before eventually being used by an estate agent.

Continue walking down Church Road past more shops built in the 1960s and stop by the gate to Maxwell Place (Stop 4). Make sure you read the plaque on the wall which explains the reasons for the name. What the plaque doesn't tell you is that here we are entering the oldest part of the village. Before Evelyn Cottages were built, excavations by Cotswold Archaeology in 2003 and 2004 found ditches and pits mostly dating to the Middle Iron Age (*c.*400BC-*c.*100BC). They were conclusively

Cotswold Archaeology excavations at Maxwell Place

linked with the field boundaries and occupation evidence found at Gilders Paddock (See stop 9). The few sherds of Romano-British and Anglo-Saxon pottery (*c.*5th century AD to 9th century AD) suggested the site was less intensively used during these periods but the remains of a possible 12th-century stone building together with a large number of rubbish pits (no wheelie bins then!) marked its redevelopment in the Later Middle Ages. This and any other later medieval buildings had been demolished by the early 18th century, leaving the site as garden until the building of Evelyn Cottages.

Now look back and compare the view with a photograph taken *c.*1972. The telegraph pole provides a reference point. The nearer

The Cottage Loaf and former engine house. The sign for petrol indicates Oldacres' garage stood behind these buildings

white building housed Bishop's Cleeve's fire engine until January 1924 when the building was sold and the engine was moved to the Tithe Barn. Charlie Trapp lived in the main building and in 1911 he was paid £1.2s.6d. (£1.12½p) for looking after the engine, reporting in that year it had attended three rick and one cottage fire. By 1927 his pay had increased to £5 a year as 'captain of the fire engine'. On the outbreak of a fire the first thing he had to do was to catch the horses to

The old fire engine at the Tithe Barn

pull it! Ernie Freebury remembered its being used when Oldacre's mill caught fire in April 1931. Later that year the parish council entered an agreement with Cheltenham's fire brigade to provide a fire engine at an annual cost of £9. The old engine was not used again and in 1941 the chief fire officer said he could not recommend its being used and prohibited its taking of water from the mains. At that time it was said to have been 110 years old, needed ten men to operate it and could throw a fifty foot jet of water, but it never seems to have been very efficient. It was extensively overhauled in October 1916 but just three months later the operators complained it leaked and soaked them whenever they used it! In 1943 it was offered to Cheltenham museum but the offer was refused.

In the photograph also notice the adjoining thatched cottage, another one which belonged to a half-yardlander. In 1839 a malthouse stood behind it which probably indicated it was then being used as a beer house. The malthouse belonged to the glebe and was demolished in 1890. When the photograph was taken the cottage housed a tea room called the Cottage Loaf. After suffering a disastrous fire in 1972 it was demolished four years together with the Spinning Wheel and replaced by the shops of Mill Parade. The millennium garden stands partly on

This view from the top of St Michael's tower in 1992 shows the extent of Oldacres' mill

this site. Interestingly the Spinning Wheel later stood on the site of the village's slaughter house which had been demolished in the 1890s. All this area belonged to the glebe in 1839.

Stop next opposite the entrance to Tesco (Stop 5). This was once the entrance to Oldacres' mill. The Oldacre story is an interesting one and is told in *Case Study 1*. The only visual evidence that the mill existed is its former showroom and office block (but not the top storey!) to the left of the entrance to Tesco's carpark, built in 1961.

The arrival of Tesco has been the most significant recent development in the historic village centre, yet it was not universally welcomed at the time. Despite an intense publicity campaign by the company, pointing out that over 60% of the villagers' shopping was carried out in Cheltenham and that the store would provide 200 jobs for local people, the villagers voted by 1200 votes to 700 against its arrival. Therefore many felt betrayed when Tewkesbury Borough Council allowed the development to go ahead. Judging by the popularity of the store today, many objectors might just have reconsidered their original objections.

However, a positive outcome of the building of the store proved to be the opportunities in 1998 and again in 2004 it gave for archaeologists

Developing the Tesco site in July 1998

from Wessex Archaeology to increase our understanding of the village's earliest history. A single hole into which a wooden post once stood, approximately in the middle of Aisle 15 inside the supermarket, indicated people were living in this part of the village centre in the Early Bronze Age (*c.*2500BC-*c.*1500BC). Halfway down what is now the delivery road for lorries, post holes of two round houses, one twelve metres in diameter, the other eight metres, provided clear evidence people were living here in the Middle Iron Age (*c.*400BC-*c.*100BC) at the same time as at 21 Church Road and at Gilders Paddock. Ditches were cut and re-cut throughout the Romano-British (43AD-410AD) and Anglo-Saxon (410AD-1066AD) periods until the site seems to have been abandoned in the 13th century, as people moved further up what is now Church Road. It is in this part of the village that sufficient evidence has been found to

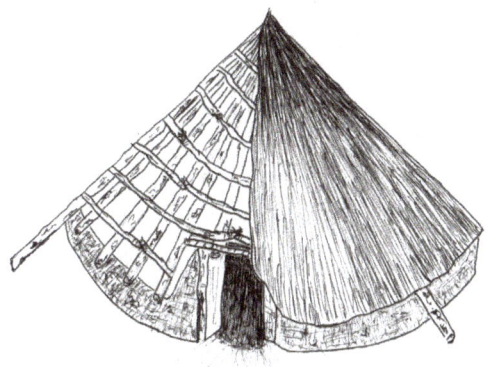
Artist's impression of an Iron Age roundhouse

allow the archaeologists to conclude that people have lived here in Bishop's Cleeve without a break since at least the Bronze Age.

Take care to cross the road, stop just past the King's Head to compare the pre-1909 photograph with today's scene (Stop 6). On the

The village green with maypole before the war memorial was built

right the King's Head, another medieval building, has been selling beer for many years. In 1851 it was recorded as a beer house run by Ann Little; in 1889 it was still being run by her sister Sarah. But what a transformation opposite! The maypole stands on the village green. The 17th-century cottages shown in the photograph have also disappeared, replaced in the early 1960s by a row of shops. It was the poor condition of these and similar cottages in the 1950s which largely prompted the county planning officer in September 1956 to recommend to the parish council that about twenty old houses 'in the low category' be demolished. From this recommendation Church Road developed as the commercial centre of the village with lock-up shops built from re-constituted Cotswold stone. One of these was the village post office which in 1961 replaced the earlier post office just seen on the left of the photograph.

The next stop is in the car park of the Tithe Barn and here you are standing in the remains of a farmyard attached to the manor house of the Bishop of Worcester, which is now Cleeve Hall (Stop 7). The Tithe Barn was built *c.*1475 to store the produce of the land for the

The Tithe Barn c.1885 with the rector Benjamin Hemming

bishop's use and for sale, although archaeologists now think it might have been built on the site of an earlier timber-framed barn. We know the date because timbers for the roof were brought in that year from the bishop's parkland at his country residence at Hartlebury. They would have come down the River Severn to Tewkesbury. It only became a tithe barn for storing the tithes given to the rector of St Michael's, when the then rector, Timothy Gates, bought the manor of Cleeve, including the bishop's manor house and its farmyard with 486a (203ha) of land, in 1624 for £3000, a huge sum at that time (it would have paid for 60,000 days' work of skilled craftsmen!). The complex had passed from the Bishop of Worcester to the Crown in 1561 and had been sold on several times before being purchased by Timothy. In 1886-87 the southern part of the barn was demolished and although the remaining part continued in use, its fabric became neglected. Other features in the farmyard, a saw pit, pond and pig sties which stood close to the road, had been cleared away by 1900. However, as the village grew with the arrival of Smiths

The dismantling of the southern end of the Tithe Barn showing the cruck construction of the roof. The barn was being built in 1475 and therefore crucks were being used in construction at that date

This commemorative sketch shows the Tithe Barn on its opening as a village hall in 1956 with the now demolished bike shed converted from the old farm buildings

Industries, in October 1946 the rector, Reverend Thomas Jesson, agreed in principle to its conversion into the village hall. The parish council bought the barn for £500 in 1949. Seven years later it was opened as the village hall after restoration and conversion which had cost £16,000; Smiths Industries making a grant of £5000. In 2011 the glass fronted extension, which partly recreated the original length of the barn, was opened.

Now turn around to face Cleeve Hall which served as the rectory from 1624 to 1972. The main part of the building dates from *c.*1300. The date of 1667 above the porch indicates the date when the porch and the front between the two wings were added. Gothic windows were installed in the early 19th century. When Bovis Homes (now Vistry) took it over as their regional headquarters in 1998, their large extension at the back provided archaeologists with the opportunity to make significant Romano-British discoveries as mentioned earlier. You can read much more about Cleeve Hall in *Case Study 2*.

It is easy to miss the plain single-storeyed Cotswold stone building to the left of the entrance to Cleeve Hall. It had been the stables which were converted in 1947 to be the village's first permanent doctors' surgery, the idea of Dr Spiridion from Winchcombe in the year before the National Health Service was created. As the village has grown since that time a much larger surgery was built behind it in Stoke Road in what had once been the rector's kitchen garden, complete with its greenhouses. Across the junction with Stoke Road, Willow Cottage is a fine example of a seventeenth-century timber-framed dwelling. Don't ignore the historic finger post which stands here, as the shadow of 'Cleeve station' can still be made out. The station was nearly in Stoke Orchard. It had been opened in 1843 but had so few passengers that it was closed in 1950. The post itself was erected some time after 1935 when the Town Pool for washing cart wheels and horses' hoofs was filled in and the grass plot on which the post stands was created. Water which had flowed through the pool ran down the side of Stoke Road until it was culverted in 1944. Residents and travellers along the road had long complained it had become little more than an open sewer in which human waste could be seen floating down past the houses. As long ago as 1451 people were making similar complaints. Change sometimes comes very slowly.

Cleeve railway station seen under the Stoke Road railway bridge in the late nineteenth century

The trail continues back at the Tesco roundabout, but if you have time it is worth a short walk along Stoke Road to Slaney's Row, also called Dog Kennel Row, a historic reminder that it was built next to the rectory's dog kennels. It forms the only example of nineteenth-century industrial building in the village. In 1834 Richard Slaney was recorded as owning a brick works. Sometime before 1839 he built six houses for his workers. A little further along the road at Lake View Court lies a lake formed in the pit from which the clay was dug. As you walk back to the main road, notice on your right Woodbine Cottage, the white painted, thatched timber-framed house at right angles to the road. Although probably only dating from the 1600s it represents the last vestiges of the layout of a medieval extension of the village as the population grew until the early 14th century. This was South Town and we know quite a lot about it from the archaeological excavations carried out by Cotswold Archaeology in 1997 where Stoke Park Close now stands. The pottery indicated people were living here from the 12th to the 14th century. Professor Christopher Dyer of Leicester University has added to the archaeological knowledge from the archives of the Bishop of Worcester. Regularly spaced plots were laid out along what is now Stoke Road for cotlanders who held six acres (2½ha) or mondaymen, who held three acres (1¼ha). Professor Dyer thinks the mondaymen may have been the descendants of the slaves recorded in Domesday Book in 1087. Slavery had been abolished a century later and it would have made sense to provide the former slaves with small plots of land for their own use conveniently close to the bishop's manor house so his officials could keep an eye on them. Obliged to work just one day a week to pay for their holding, they were free on the other days to work as paid labourers. Both they and the cotlanders obviously needed to find paid work to provide the necessities of life. A document of 1393-94, nearly half a century after the Black Death, tells us that only six of the twenty one similar plots across the whole village were still occupied and the buildings on the empty plots were falling into ruin. The bishop did not like this as it meant he was less likely to be able to rent out the abandoned plots in the future. As an example, in October 1412 Juliana Hone was ordered to repair her ruinous buildings, but in January 1413 she handed them back to the bishop, presumably as she was not in a position to repair them. At the end of that century in October 1490 five tenants were ordered to repair their buildings, in April 1491 another seven were given the same order and in October 1503 five. The fact that the plots did become abandoned suggests the bishop's officials did not have great success in preventing decline. You can read more about these development in the extension walk along Station Road and Priory Lane. As you walk back to the main road, the small Cotswold stone cottages you pass were built for farm labourers about the same time as Slaney's Row, but most of the plots remained paddocks and orchards until the 1950s, since when there has been infilling.

 Retrace your steps towards the roundabout, cross at the traffic lights. Look across the road at the narrow alley which now leads to The Withers modern development, but which led formerly to fields. Skilly Alley doesn't look much today but you wouldn't have wanted to have walked along it at times in the past. In 1910 the parish council complained young men were causing a nuisance along it. The local policeman had to be called in 1926 to deal with youthful anti-social behaviour and again, but more seriously, in 1943 and 1944 when American soldiers from the war-time camp in Gotherington Lane were accused of accosting local girls in the alley. The camp commander declared he had no idea that had been happening!

Once outside the King's Head compare the present view with the view from a postcard posted in 1927 (Stop 8). At that time this stretch

Looking north past the war memorial

of Cheltenham Road could claim to be the commercial centre of the village. There was a butcher and shoe repairer and the buildings on the right belonged to the blacksmith's forge which in 1839 had been used as a wheelwright's shop. The photograph was taken just before Joe Powers opened his cycle repair shop near the far junction which he turned into the village's first petrol station, selling 'motor spirit' by filling the motorists' own cans. In the far distance stood Rose Villa, another early 19th century house with pretensions. In 1861 and again in 1927 the curate of St Michael's church was living there but in 1937 it was bought by Joe Powers. It was demolished when the Cleeveview estate was built in the early 1960s, yet the gateway, although now hidden, still stands as evidence for its existence. Home Farm stood behind the wall on the left of the photograph; this wall and the farm house survive but not the farm buildings which were swept away for Budgen's supermarket in

Joe Power's petrol station

Budgen's supermarket in 1995

1990. When Tesco arrived in 1998 Budgen's could not compete and Lidl's now stands on the site. In 2020 the present building was opened having demolished the original building as it was considered too small. Many villagers have regretted these modern developments in and around the historic village centre but the archaeology which the developments have produced have added immensely to our understanding of the history of the village. Walk along Cheltenham Road to Gilders Paddock (Stop 9).

There is nothing to see now but when Charles Parry of the Gloucestershire Excavation Unit led an archaeological dig in 1989 in the paddocks of The Old Farm which existed here before the houses were built, it soon became obvious that he had discovered an area of ditches, indicating small paddocks, and pits dating back to the Iron Age. The pottery indicated this area had been in use from the 4th century BC to the 1st century AD. More excitingly the skeletons of four adults and three children were discovered. Dated to the 3rd or 4th century AD they remain the earliest known residents of Bishop's Cleeve. Taken with the Tesco site and that at Maxwell Place in Church Road, Gilders Paddock indicated an area of Iron Age activity lying under this western edge of the present village centre. The evidence showed that people lived by keeping livestock - cattle, sheep, goats and growing crops such as wheat, barley, oats, rye and peas. Now turn around. When the yard at Home Farm was developed for Budgen's supermarket in 1993-94, archaeologists from Cotswold Archaeology made more major discoveries; fragments of Bronze Age, Iron Age and Romano-British pottery, evidence of metal working in the 2nd century AD and bread ovens form the 3rd and 4th centuries AD. Then sometime between 300AD and 400AD the ditches were abandoned and a large quantity of rubble from a high status building was spread across the site. The quantity of Romano-British material led Charles Parry to suggest people had 'moved across the road' from the area of Gilders Paddock by the middle of the 2nd century AD, which then allowed that ground to be used for the burials. Crucially eighteen

One of the skeletons found at Gilder's Paddock in 1989

fragments of Anglo-Saxon pottery, probably from the 5th to 7th centuries indicated that life had continued through what is still known by many people as the 'Dark Ages'. As outlined in the *Introduction*, the area from Cleeve Hall to Home Farm was an area of settlement in the pre-historic and Romano-British periods, and perhaps influenced some of the shape of the historic village in the Anglo-Saxon period.

Carefully cross the road and stop at the corner of Cheltenham Road and Station Road (Stop 10). You are standing at Gilder's corner, named after William Gilder who was farming here in 1901. As long ago as 1926 the county council proposed a bypass to avoid this very awkward corner but it took another seventy years before it was opened. William had been born in nearby Woolstone and his wife Ellen in Staverton, but the seven sons and two daughters had all been born in Bishop's Cleeve. Before you turn up Station Road let your eye follow the fencing westwards until it comes to the timber-framed building at right angles to the road. This is another example of a cruck construction. The old road to Evesham turns right just past the cottage and runs through another medieval extension of the village, called Newtown, a name which was still in use in the first decade of the last century, although the plots had probably been abandoned at the same time as the plots in Stoke Road. They would have been completely forgotten if the building of the Willow Park Drive estate had not revealed fragments of medieval cooking pots still resting on what had once been hearths.

If you do walk round to Newtown, don't be misled into thinking Cleeveway Manor was another traditional manor because that name is quite a recent one. Nevertheless the Cleeveway is an impressive building probably dating to before the 18th century with 19th-century additions. You can read more about it in *Case Study 3*.

Before walking up Station Road you might wonder what the road was called before the station opened in 1906. At various times it was called Woodmancote Road or Lane, but it was also called Slades Lane. The Slades can be found on Nottingham Hill which might indicate an earlier destination for the route than Woodmancote. Now walk up Station Road and stop at the entrance to Shipway Court, built by Tewkesbury Borough Council in 1971 and named after the family who owned the field on which it was built (Stop 11). Opposite stands The Old Farm, the most ostentatious timber-framed building in the whole village. Notice

The Old Farm in 2007 when the floods re-established the stream which flowed down this part of Station Road and fed the rector's fishponds. The stream was recorded on the 1839 Tithe map

how much closer together the timbers are than the other timber-framed houses in the village. So who might have built it? Probably an upwardly-mobile Thomas Yardington or his son, also Thomas. Thomas senior was recorded as a cotlander in 1475 with 6a (2½ha) of land, but from 1471 to 1525 he rented the Bishop of Worcester's demesne. The demesne extended to 400a (160 ha); a very large area. Thomas's increasing standing in the village is shown by the fact he served at different times as the village reeve, the bishop's bailiff and as a juror at the bishop's manor court. Whether as reeve or bailiff he was responsible for the smooth running of the bishop's manor. After paying his workers and selling the produce, the demesne was obviously so profitable that when his son Thomas succeeded him he described himself as a 'yeoman' - a term of status. The architecture indicates the house was built before 1500, announcing that Thomas senior had greatly increased his status in the village. Its position was also significant, built on a 'green field' site away from the heart of the village and turning its back on the more humble homes along Church Road. It is even possible it was built at the end of the rectory garden which we know in 1392 bordered the fishponds which lay on the line of Station Road. Perhaps the Tithe Barn was re-built as part of the deal between Thomas and the bishop. Bishop John Alcock (1476-86) is known to have invested in rebuilding his barns.

As you walk on you would never guess that the yard behind The Old Farm housed a small racing stable until the 1960s. A century ago it was run by Arthur Saxby, a jockey who rode around 300 winners during his career. In his history of the village, Ernie Freebury recounts that Billy Stott, who rode Golden Miller to win the Cheltenham Gold Cup in 1933, also trained here. During his career Billy rode over 600 winners. In 1963 a young stable girl with the name Jenny Harvey arrived. She left after two years and soon after, at the age of nineteen, married Richard Pitman. Jenny Pitman was the first female trainer to win the Grand National, with Corbière in 1983. In 1991 she had success with the locally-owned horse, Garrison Savannah, in the Cheltenham Gold Cup. The feat is commemorated in the Garrison Savannah suite behind the King's Head public house which you passed earlier. Jenny won both races twice before retiring from horse training in 1998 to become a very successful writer of novels with a horse racing theme. The village has a long connection with horse racing and not just because its public houses provide a convenient staging post for today's racegoers.

Another famous person associated with The Old Farm was the actor Robert Hardy who died in 2017. The history books state he was born in the village, but they are wrong! When he was born in 1925 his father, Major Henry Hardy, was headmaster of Cheltenham College and the family was living in College House in Thirlestaine Road in Cheltenham. Henry was headmaster from 1919 to 1932 before he moved to Shrewsbury School from where he retired to The Old Farm

This view from St Michael's tower in the early 1960s not only shows the stables and paddocks behind The Old Farm but also Home Farm and the early development of the Cleeveview estate. In the distance can be seen Cleevelands Cottage and the regular-shaped fields created at enclosure and now built upon

in 1944; he died in 1958. Robert was aged nineteen and a student at Oxford University when his mother and father moved here. He also served for a spell in the RAF during the Second World War. His acting career spanned from 1956 to 2017 and one of his most famous rôles was Cornelius Fudge, the Minister for Magic, in the Harry Potter films. He was also an expert on the long bow and was involved in the restoration and interpretation of the Mary Rose, Henry VIII's famous ship, raised in 1982 and displayed at Portsmouth.

First recorded in 1855, this part of Bishop's Cleeve was known as 'The Street'; the home of 'the quality'. Perhaps not surprisingly, therefore, this stretch of road to Gotherington Lane was the first in the village to be sprayed with tar to reduce the dust in 1926. As you walk up the road you pass Southfield on the left - a fine early 19th-century house. In 1927 a gardener/chauffeur, maid and daily help were employed there. In 1883 the *Cheltenham Examiner* reported that workmen digging a sand pit on the opposite side of the road to Southfield found a grave which contained a body with pottery dating from the Romano-British period. The pottery included an amphora jar of the sort which was usually used to bring oil and wine from southern Europe. Unfortunately that is all we know about the find. In the Later Middle Ages this area was the rector's orchard, and possibly vineyard, but then in the 19th century it was used as a sandpit and subsequently the village rubbish dump. Houses were built on the site in the 1970s. Now walk on and stop at the entrance to Sandown Road (Stop 12).

Sandown Road leads into the Cleeveview estate, started in 1962 on the land of Cleeveland's farm. This was a 250 acre (100ha) farm bought by Oldacres from Fred Minett in 1942 for £5000 (approximately £240K today – how land prices have increased since then!). By 1962 Oldacres had purchased much of the farmland to the north of the village; land upon which the village has greatly expanded since 1980. Look carefully to your left at the first part of the Cotswold stone wall at the junction with

Jack Minett stands outside Cleevelands Farm (now 23 and 25 Station Road) in 1921

Sandown Road and there is just enough remaining limewash to serve as a reminder of the barn which was demolished when Sandown Road was built through the former farmyard. The farmhouse is now 23 and 25 Station Road; brick-built facing the road but still timber-framed on its eastern side. It appears to be an interesting building and indeed it is. The style of the brickwork suggests this is one of the oldest brick walls in the village, dating back to the early 17th century, if not before, and built of local clay, probably taken from along Stoke Road. It would have replaced the original timber-framing. As the wall faces south it is exposed to the extremes of the weather. The south-facing wall of The Old Farm has been similarly affected, but not the north-facing wall which lies in the shadows and so avoids the extremes of the summer and winter weather. The wall here masks a greater antiquity, for the building is based on five pairs of crucks, which suggest a date in the later 15th century if not earlier. Its position is also significant, standing almost opposite The Priory - the original rectory, despite its modern name. Part might even have its origins as a rectory barn. You can read about The Priory in *Case Study 4*. Look carefully and you will notice the road is somewhat lower than the surrounding gardens, for here were the rector's three fishponds, two small and one large, recorded in 1396-97. The stream of water which fed into them was only culverted between the Old Manor House and Gilder's corner in 1837. It is even shown on the 1839 Tithe map, the surveying for which here had taken place before the stream was culverted. Before then villagers using the footpath out of the churchyard had to cross the stream by stepping stones. You can read more about this footpath in the walk around St Michael's church.

    Now continue along Station Road passing a terrace of early 19th-century labourers' cottages, one of which was licensed by Thomas Staite in 1841 as the first meeting house for Methodists. Stop just past The Old Manor House (Stop 13). It is clearly another house of 'the quality' and in 1927 a gardener/handyman and maid were employed there. Greater detail can be found in *Case Study 5*. Turn round to the horse chestnut tree on the island at the junction of Station Road and School Road. Long-established villagers know this as the James Browning memorial tree. Presented to the village in 1909 by James Browning, who was the landlord of Saint George's Vaults, next to the library in Cheltenham, it

left: The narrow finger of grass alongside the pavement has been here for over one hundred years – a rare survivor

was originally planted on what was then the village green, now Tesco's roundabout. When the site was chosen for the war memorial after the Great War it was quite a challenging task to move the tree to this location. The timber work on the black and white house called The Old Cottage at the corner of Gotherington Lane indicates it was built before c.1550. It was recorded as a carpenter's shop in 1839

If you wish to follow the extended walk continue up Station Road to Stop A; otherwise cross the road into School Road (Stop 14).

The modern houses on the left mask an interesting history. They were built on the site of a small Methodist chapel on land behind Yew Tree House in Station Road in 1899. When the congregation declined the building was sold to the Women's Institute in 1934. With the arrival of newcomers to the Smiths' estate, services re-started in 1951 until a new chapel was opened in Bishop's Close on Smiths' estate in 1959, although the Sunday School continued to meet here for a few more years. In 1964 the site was acquired for a new Roman Catholic church, the St John Fisher Hall. Before then the congregation had held their services in the Tithe Barn. Thirty five years later problems with the structure led to its closure in 2000 when its congregation returned to worship in St Michael's church, as it had done before the Reformation. Moving on to Priory Lane, where the extension trail rejoins the main trail, the house on the nearer corner

The former Methodist chapel and behind it the St John Fisher hall before its closure in 2000

was recorded as a grocer's shop in 1851 and 1861. Note that the house on the farther corner carries a date 1817 but there are no records that it was once a mill. Continue along School Road.

The date on the name plate at Church View conveniently gives 1850 as the date of its construction but it probably replaced an earlier building shown on the Tithe Map of 1839. In 1927 it was serving as the village police station. The double doors almost opposite today lead into a private garden, but during the 19th century they led to the village pound where animals caught roaming were impounded until the owner claimed them by paying a small fee. If we can presume the pound here had a long history, in May 1451 it was reported at the bishop's court that it contained seven sheep, a pig and six piglets. In October 1468 only a single horse was reported. It seems to have gone out of use in the 1930s. The semi-detached bungalows next to St Michael's Centre replaced another decaying timber-framed house in the late 1960s but the timber-framed house opposite does survive, although it has been much extended in recent years. The original part, seen from the pound, stands at right angles to the road. In 1914 it was the only place in the village where villagers could consult a doctor. Richard Davies, who was the doctor for Cheltenham workhouse, attended here on Tuesdays and Fridays at 12.30pm. Then in the 1950s it served as the school tuck shop. Its position in the churchyard indicates it was very probably built as a church house and used to provide an income for the church in the Later Middle Ages through holding church or parish ales – general festivities with music, dancing and drinking. In 1589 it was described as being well-kept, but in 1635 it was reported as being in urgent need of repair. This was probably the consequence of the church ales having died out by that date. There is a similar cottage by the church in Swindon Village. Your next stop is in front of St Michael's Centre (Stop 15). Until 1842 this marked the end of what is now School Road as only a footpath ran from here towards the village centre. The records tell us the churchyard wall was built in that year.

In 1846 the rector of Bishop's Cleeve, the Reverend William Lawrence Townsend, together with a number of subscribers, opened a National School for 'the education of the poor in the Principles of the Established Church of England and Wales'. In practice the subscribers intended to teach the children to look up to and obey their 'betters'

The Reverend William Lawrence Townsend in old age. He was still rector when he died in Cheltenham aged 85

and not indulge in petty anti-social behaviour. Built of stone from Cleeve Hill, the only view the school children had from the windows was of St Michael's church itself! At that time education was neither free nor compulsory but when it opened 69 children attended day school and another 46 on Sundays but 53 attended neither. Unfortunately we don't know how regular the attendances were. When it closed in 1874 because the subscribers' contributions were insufficient to keep the school going, the running was taken over by an elected secular Board of Education. In 1905 an extension to the south was built for the infants. At various times during the Second World War the school educated evacuees from

Pupils at the school in 1924

as far away as Birmingham, Eastbourne and London. Most only stayed a few weeks before returning home and of the 112 children evacuated throughout the war, at the close of the war in 1945, only five remained on the register. A year earlier it was recorded that 241 children were on the register. As the village grew with the arrival of Smiths Industries temporary classrooms were created in the grounds. In 1953 two new

The school in 1972 showing some of the increased accommodation around the original building

classrooms were constructed because the number of children arriving at the school was 78 but only 28 were leaving. In 1956 a secondary modern school was built in Two Hedges Road for the older pupils. This was the origin of the present Cleeve School. After the primary school completed its removal to its present location in Tobyfield Road in 1981, Rectory Court and Churchfields were built on the site and the stone-built school building became St Michael's Centre reverting to the church according to a stipulation when it was built. Now move on to the war memorial site (Stop 17).

You are now standing on the site of the two cottages in the photograph, demolished in 1966. There was just enough surviving

Cottages on the present site of the war memorial which were demolished when the road was straightened

evidence to identify the nearer cottage as another cruck-framed building; part of the Cheapside area of the village. An earlier entrance into St Michael's church yard once existed where the road makes a right-angled turn, but it is now completely blocked by more recent buildings. The 1839 Tithe map shows the path in the churchyard making for this entrance but it was already blocked by a garden. If you look carefully you will notice that the front of Gothic Cottage, which you have just passed, faces this old entrance to the churchyard. As the war memorial was being moved here in 1980 unfortunately the Royal Engineers responsible for

The restored war memorial was re-dedicated by the Bishop of Gloucester in September 2018

the move broke the shaft and so shortened it. To commemorate the centenary of the end of the Great War, the memorial was repaired and re-dedicated in September 2018 after the parish council had spent £12,000 on the restoration.

It is worth studying the names to discover those families who still live in the village. When parishes decided to build war memorials to commemorate their fallen after the end of the Great War, there was no official guidance about selecting the names. There are 55 names on this war memorial but only 21 were living in Bishop's Cleeve or Woodmancote at the time they enlisted. A further eleven came from Gotherington and Southam, which are still in the church's parish but have their own memorials. This means that some names appear on two memorials. Vyvyan Coupland-Smith is commemorated here, at Southam and also Cheltenham. Nine are also commemorated on graves in the churchyard and three more are only recorded on graves in the churchyard; not on the war memorial. You can read about the Eagar brothers in *Case Study 4*. Only eleven names were added from the Second World War, serving as a reminder of the changed nature of warfare between the two world wars.

Egremont was replaced by this building which started life as a restaurant before becoming an office block. Seen here in 1995 it was later demolished and replaced by Aston Court

Next turn to look down Tobyfield Road. On your left is Aston Court built on the site of Egremont Villa, which was demolished in 1991. On the opposite side of Tobyfield Road the present dentists' surgery was built as a police station *c.*1860 on the site of an old barn. The two large shops were built on the site of Edginton's bakery which stood along Tobyfield Road from 1830 to 1953. In 1891 the address of the bakery was given as Cheapside and so here also it's fitting that the two shops are continuing to trade in the area where medieval shops once stood. The bakery building was demolished in 1968. Your final stop is by the entrance to the library and school, where the old village meets the new (Stop 17).

In front of you stand three pairs of semi-detached houses, much enlarged compared to their original size. They were built by Cheltenham Rural District Council in 1947 on the site of the farmhouse of Tobyfield farm, recorded in 1851 as a small farm of 10 acres (4ha). These semis represent part of the last building phase before modern Bishop's Cleeve began to grow with the laying out of Tobyfield Road and the building by Taylor Woodrow of what became known as Smiths' estate for the Bishop's Cleeve Housing Association, partly funded by the national government, which started in 1948. The estate was designed by T.P.Bennett architects of Bloomsbury in London. Smiths Industries and Cheltenham Rural District Council worked together to build 478 houses and 10 shops between 1948 and 1954. Look along Tobyfield Road towards the red brick houses of that estate – it was the forerunner of the many estates which have subsequently fanned out from the historic centre, completely changing the nature and size of the village. If you have time to explore the estate you will discover it was built on Garden City principles with plenty of open space and many ornamental trees, but built when accommodating the motorcar was not seen as a priority - only 227 garages were built; fewer than one for every two houses. Today the original garage blocks have given way to housing and front gardens have been turned into drives for the cars. Notice that Tobyfield Lane lies between the school and Tobyfield Road. This is the last surviving remnant of the road to Cheltenham before the existing road past the

Edginton's bakery c.1925

racecourse was built as a turnpike road in 1810. The new road proved much more convenient than this old route which took the traveller to Cheltenham via Two Hedges Road, Southam and Prestbury and so the old route was blocked off in 1848 although a footpath continued to follow its line until the building of Smiths' estate. Note on the right of the lane the timber-framed cottage called Little Croft, which dates back to at least the 1600s. In 1851 Isaac Courtier, a shepherd, lived here with his wife Sarah and two children. Together with a similar cottage, now demolished, on the opposite side of the lane, it marked the edge of the historic village centre. Turn next along the drive to the school. The school was first opened in 1965 when the infants moved from the old school in School Road. Bear right before reaching the school building and continue between the building provided by Tesco for community use in 1990, and the library which moved here from the Tithe Barn in 1965. If you have time to go in, you can learn much more about the history of the village. Finally walk carefully through the car park to complete this walk through the history of Bishop's Cleeve.

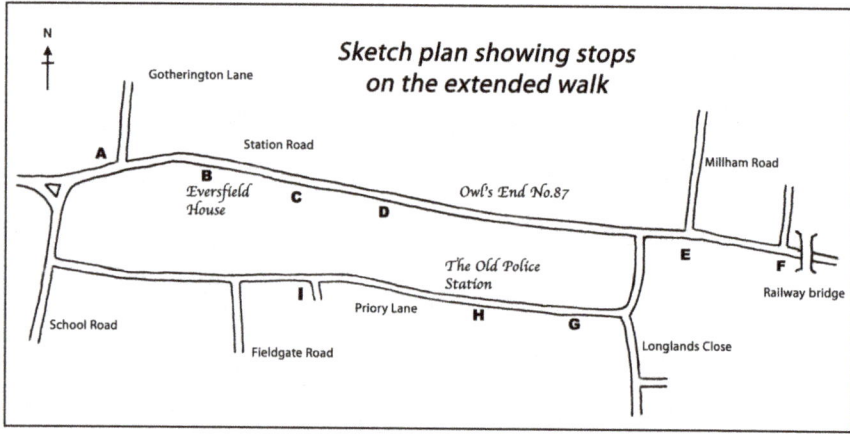

right: Station Road and Priory Lane in 1883. Notice how the Woodmancote parish boundary is marked by stones at The Throughts. Taken from the 1883 25-inch Ordnance Survey map (National Library of Scotland)

EXTENDED WALK ALONG STATION ROAD AND PRIORY LANE

THIS EXTENSION takes you to an area of the village which was created as the population grew until the early 14th century. It was called *Bovetoun* - 'above town' - and first recorded in 1299 but probably laid out in the preceding century. The laying out of what is now Station Road and Priory Lane seems to have created a green lying between them.

It was developed for the cotlanders with their 6a (2½ha) holdings. In 1299 thirteen tenants were recorded as living here but then some of the homes were abandoned as the population fell after the Black Death 1348-49 and shrinkage set in. A century or so later in 1475 only one inhabited cottage but seven empty plots were recorded and in 1514 the ruinous buildings were too numerous to list. This led to many of the regularly spaced plots being amalgamated, as can be seen on nineteenth-century maps. It is possible the three surviving timber-framed buildings

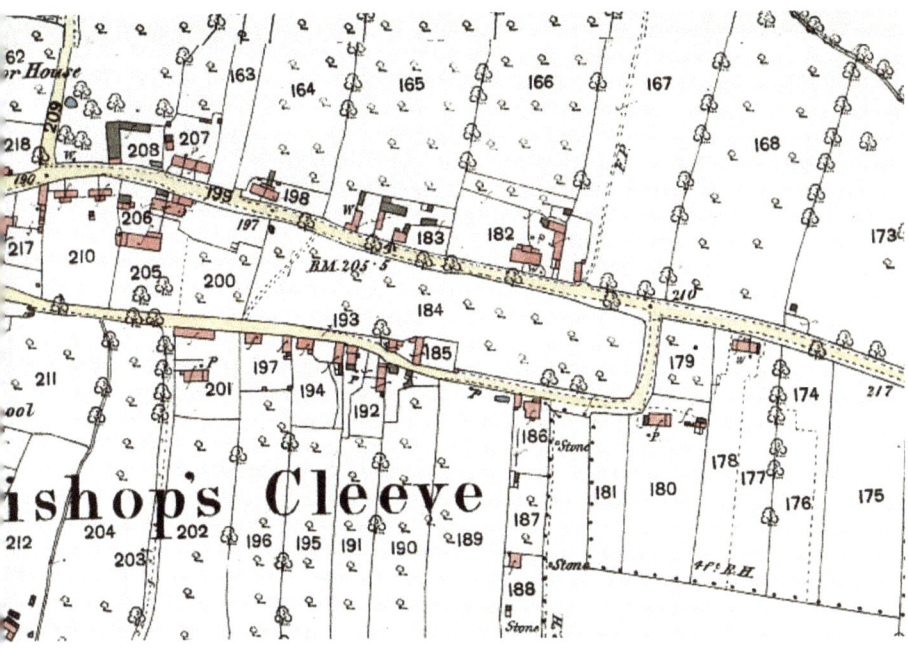

on this walk were constructed in the 17th century on these amalgamated plots and after the original buildings had fallen into ruin. As the village expanded again in the early 19th and 20th centuries the empty plots were gradually filled. So there are many layers to be unwrapped as you follow the route.

Stop first at the Gotherington Road junction (Stop A). Behind you stands the most imposing early 19th century brick-built house in the village. Its origins are uncertain but in my history of Bishop's Cleeve I erroneously suggested it had been the parish workhouse. It's difficult to imagine now that until the present century the house next to it immediately opposite the end of Gotherington Lane, 44 Station Road, served this part of the village as a general store; its closing another casualty of the rise of the supermarkets. On this site, if not in

Priory Stores, known to locals as Jeanes' shop

this actual house, it was here in 1851 that little Arthur Chew was living with his widowed father and three siblings. At nine years old he was the youngest person in the village to be described as an agricultural labourer in the census of that year. Forty four per cent of the village's employed population was recorded as agricultural labourers in the census, by far the largest occupation. Now take a look down Gotherington Lane where the Homelands estate has been developed since the 1990s. In the distance you can see the roundabout at the end of Sunrise Avenue which runs in from the left. The avenue runs through the site of the US Army camp of the Second World War. Older villagers can still recall the tragic incident which took place near the camp in March 1944 which led to two black American soldiers being hanged for raping a local girl who had been going home after a village dance accompanied by a white American soldier, whom they knocked unconscious. Just out of sight on the right before the roundabout lies Oldacre Drive, built in the mid 1970s, which commemorates the family who owned the land on which the Homelands estate has been built.

The next two stone-built houses on the right have as their origins the Bishop's Cleeve poorhouse. In 1801 Bishop's Cleeve vestry paid £200 for a property to house the poor, the old, infirm, single mothers, orphans and the unemployed, who were not able to fend for themselves or exist within their own homes on the small sums of money and provisions provided by the parish overseers. These were unpaid officials from the village who served a year at a time to distribute the income from the Poor Law rates levied on the village's houses. In 1836 the building was sold to help meet the costs of setting up a much larger Union workhouse in Winchcombe to which the local paupers were supposed to enter to receive poor relief, because a harsher, more punitive system had been set up by an Act of Parliament in 1834. The present houses were then built on the site sometime before 1883, possibly incorporating earlier features. As you move on compare the view with that recorded c.1910 by the photograph overleaf. Notice that the barn on the left has been demolished and houses built on the site.

Walk on to Eversfield House (Stop B). The story of Eversfield House's tea and pleasure grounds is told in *Case Study 6*. The oldest part of the house is that which fronts the pavement. Crucks were used in its roof timbers but they look as if they have been re-used, possibly from one of the decaying original buildings of *Bovetoun*. However the rest of the house is late 17th or early 18th century and the scar of a roof apex indicates that there have been alterations. The extension on the right was used as a bakery until 1987. This is the rear of the house; its front and garden face Priory Lane. It has similarities with The Priory and so

Station Road c.1910 before the surface was tarmaced

dates from about the same period, but unfortunately nothing more is known about its origins. However its location suggests it was built on deserted plots of *Bovetoun*. The terrace of three neatly-kept farm labourers' cottages on the opposite side of the road was built in the early 19th century as the population of the village began to grow slowly.

Continue up Station Road past the three detached houses on your right. When built in 1987 this was called the Eversfield Gardens development which unashamedly traded on the association with the pleasure grounds. Stop opposite Bootenhay on your left (Stop C). Today it is one house but in 1839 and 1911 it was recorded as two cottages. The earliest record of the name is in 1650 but its meaning remains a mystery, 'hay' means an enclosure but what the rest of the name means can only be guesswork. It was recorded as Boulton Hay in 1826. The archives have thrown some light on its history. In 1650 it was described as a close of pasture of 1½a (⅔ha), which was very likely two empty plots from the shrunken settlement. This would mean that at least part of the existing building was constructed some time after this date, possibly soon after. In 1798 it was said to belong to the manor of Bishop's Cleeve. In 1928 the continuing existence of a rick yard behind it indicates it has been used as a farm. An unanswered query is why the area of the medieval green extending to Priory Lane opposite was sometimes called Bootenhay Orchard, for the link is not clear. This remained an orchard until 1928 when the Denleys at Eversfield House sold it off and building began, which explains why all the houses you will pass on your right have been built since 1928, but obviously at different times. They provide some good examples of developments in 20th-century architecture, both pleasing and less so.

 Move on a little way until the medieval-styled windows of 79 Station Road come into view and stop opposite this thatched cottage, one of the three surviving timber-framed houses on this tour (Stop D). Notice how it has been built at right angles to the road as have the two other houses, probably reflecting the original orientation of the houses in *Bovetoun*, indicating the desire to fit in as many houses and farm yards as possible in narrow plots in order to accommodate the growing population with the bishop profiting from their labour services and other dues when medieval *Bovetoun* was set out. Like Bootenhay it was built on abandoned late medieval plots but unlike Bootenhay it reflects the late medieval orientation at right angles to the road. The next building of note is Owl's End, 87 Station Road, with its fine, probably late 17th or

Owl's End house, probably with Dr Soden and his car

early 18th century western wing. When Ernie Freebury wrote about life in Bishop's Cleeve in 1927 this was the home of Miss Rigby from where she ran a farm and where Dr Soden from Winchcombe attended, if you left a note for him. The only permanent medical provision at the time was provided by two district nurses, Nurses Morehen and Slade, who lived farther up Station Road in Woodmancote. They retired in 1946, two years before the setting up of the National Health Service.

Immediately after the house you will see double gates which lead into a yard. Behind them stands a single storeyed building. It is easy to walk past without noticing it, but it is an important building in the more recent history of the village. It was on this site in 1885 that Walter John Oldacre started the Oldacre business. Since 1881 he had been living at the main house and in 1885 he installed a small steam engine to grind animal feed, bringing the coal by horse and cart from Ashchurch station. So began the Oldacre business (see *Case Study 1*). Next you come to the thatched Rose Cottage, the original part of which lies at right angles to the road, which again reflects the lay out of *Bovetoun*. The earliest reference dates to c.1684 but it could be earlier and like number 79 was built after the original buildings had long decayed.

Keep walking on towards the railway bridge which since 2000 has carried the Gloucestershire Warwickshire Steam Railway across the road. Look down Millham Road (Stop E). Building here began in 1947 as part of the attempt to improve the nation's housing after the Second World War, especially in rural areas. The original houses were Airey houses, made from prefabricated reinforced concrete and named after their designer, Sir Edwin Airey. 26,000 were built nationally by local councils, in this case Cheltenham Rural District Council. They were cheap and quick to build but lacked cavity walls and over time other problems occurred so that the national government declared them all defective in 1985, since which time Tewkesbury Borough Council has rebuilt them. The name of the road is, however, much older and refers to a meadow attached to a mill. The mill has long since disappeared. As long ago as c.1170 there is a reference to an abandoned mill and in 1400 there is a further reference to a ruinous mill. So the villagers had to travel to Woodmancote for their grain to be ground, either in one of the two mills in Stockwell Lane or to the windmill between Woodmancote and Southam, until they could buy their flour and bread in shops by the early

This aerial photograph taken in 1972 shows Millham Road on the edge of the village, before the Airey houses were rebuilt

19th century. In 1413 there was reference in the bishop's manor court to Millhamend, because a ditch was ordered to be cleaned as it was causing a flood. A year later some villagers were still complaining about it.

Your final stop in Station Road is just before the railway bridge, almost at the eastern end of *Bovetoun* (Stop F). There is an interesting story behind the car showroom. The original building was built in 1935 as a shed for milking the cows on Miss Rigby's farm. Milking ceased in the early 1960s when the building became a garage selling petrol, servicing and repairing cars. This now goes on behind the present showroom which replaced the original building in the 1980s. Cross the road carefully. It is obvious why 110A has been called 'The Pines'. The trees were a feature of the stations on the original Great Western Railway line from Honeybourne to Cheltenham on which Bishop's Cleeve station

Bishop's Cleeve station shortly after it had been opened in 1906

opened in 1906. This house stands at the foot of the station approach. Next door the pair of semis was built by the railway company for the station staff, which at the opening comprised the stationmaster, two signalman, one porter and one lad porter. The stationmaster's house still stands, reached off Longlands Close. It took over 60 years for the village to gain a railway station much more convenient than Cleeve station near Stoke Orchard, but the service only lasted 54 years until it was killed off by the even more convenient, and frequent, bus services which had begun in 1923 and stopped where the entrance to Tesco now lies.

Nothing remains now to convey the importance of the station to the village in the first half of the twentieth century. Not only did thousands travel to Eversfield Tea and Pleasure Grounds by train but the first evacuees arrived here on 15 June 1940. One hundred children and five teachers from Dagenham were then taken to the school for medical examination, refreshment and the hand out of emergency ration cards. However the *Gloucestershire Echo* further reported that they were all taken by coaches out of the village to Deerhurst, Gotherington, Tewksbury, Toddington and Twyning. Even after the station closed to passengers in 1960 it continued to be used for a special purpose as both Queen Elizabeth II and her mother boarded the train here after their visits to Cheltenham races in the early 1960s.

Retrace your steps and turn left down Priory Lane which bends to the right with Longlands Close ahead of you which in turn leads to Longlands Road, houses built by Cheltenham Rural District Council starting in 1959. The close itself turns left and leads to Pine Bank which was built on the site of the station's goods yard after it closed in 1963. Keep along the lane and note how in places it still retains the atmosphere of a narrow country lane. However this masks the building and re-building which has gone on here since the Middle Ages. At least seven buildings shown on the 1839 Tithe map have disappeared beneath more recent developments. It is not known when this road was first called Priory Lane as in the 19th century it was also referred to as Woodmancote Lane. Perhaps it changed when letter writing became more popular after the introduction of the penny post in 1840 to avoid confusion with what is now Station Road.

Your first stop is on the left at the end of a seemingly never-ending drive to The Throughts, a word which means a tongue of land

A happy group of youngsters making their way from the station to Eversfield Tea Gardens in the 1920s

and which was used as an alternative name for Tobysfield when the land was farmed as strips in the early 19th century (Stop G). The fields which replaced these open strips have now themselves disappeared under 20th-century housing off Pecked Lane. What might appear amazing is that until 1953 this tongue of land was part of the parish of Woodmancote. The 1883 Ordnance Survey map even marks the boundary stones where the present drive meets the lane. In 1914 Charles Oakey worked The Throughts as a market gardener; one of six in the village as the late 19th-century depression in agriculture forced villagers to look for new opportunities, in this case supplying the village and Cheltenham with fruit and vegetables. His son Ernest was still working here in 1939 but by then the number of market gardeners had halved.

Next on your left is a cottage built in the traditional style of the first half of the 19th century, with its Cotswold stone walls, grey slate roof and rounded windows. The small stone outhouse which stands at right angles to the road is another insignificant-looking building with a story to tell, for in the late 19th century it was a blacksmith's forge. William Sollis had learnt his trade from his father in Gotherington before he moved here, probably in the 1880s. By 1901 he had retired and his forge was worked by John Prosser from Ross on Wye, who was only twenty one. The business must have ended by 1911 when the census recorded that a German couple, Felix and Anna Walther were living in the cottage. Their occupations were given as a trainer and jockey. We know Felix was working as a stud groom in Uckington ten years earlier. However they did not stay long, as happened so often in the past when most people rented rather than owned their homes.

Look carefully at the gable ends of the white block of houses on your right. Look up to find the clue that tells you they were built by Winchcombe Rural District Council in 1932, to meet the needs of local families to live in proper sanitary conditions. The rental was 6s (30p) a week, but Ernie Freebury grumbled that of the ten names of local families living in poverty which he put forward to be considered for the houses, only one was accepted. Winchcombe Rural District Council was created in 1894 and covered an area of 29 local parishes which had formed the Winchcombe Poor Law Union of 1834. Despite the vehement objections from Bishop's Cleeve and its parish council, it was disbanded in 1935 and the village found itself under Cheltenham Rural District

A reminder that the village was once part of Winchcombe Rural District Council

Council until 1974, since when it has been part of Tewkesbury Borough. They are probably the only houses in the whole of the former Winchcombe Rural District Council which carry the council's initials.

Continue along Priory Lane and stop by number 39 The Old Police Station (Stop H). The name reminds us that this was the village police station for approximately 20 years until 1953. In 1914 its name was Owls End. The plot on which it was built seems to have started life as a squatter plot on the open green, by the early 19th century at the latest. In 1839 the house was owned by Richard Yeend who lived at Bottomley Farm in Gambles Lane in Woodmancote but it appears as 'unoccupied' in the Tithe award record. It was burnt to the ground later and the present house was built as a small cottage in the early 20th century, since when it has been extended but in keeping with its country-style. In the 1930s it was the home of one of the most famous jockeys of the day, of whom you have probably never heard. Billy Speck was described as a living legend. He rode over 700 winners in a career from 1920 to 1935 and was runner-up champion jockey six times. Billy's life was tragically cut short after he fell at Cheltenham in April 1935 and died six days later in the town's hospital, at the early age of 31. Buried in Bishop's Cleeve churchyard, the local newspapers estimated the funeral procession was two miles long, but perhaps

Billy Speck's fame was recognised by his inclusion in a set of cigarette cards based on horse racing

they were emphasising his popularity rather than giving an accurate account. Now turn around and notice how some of the features of The Old Police Station are reflected in number 22a. This is probably the most imaginatively designed modern house in the village. It was built at the turn of the millennium and designed by the renowned architect Ronald Green, who had worked with Sir Hugh Casson on the design of the 1951 Festival of Britain by the River Thames in London, as older readers might remember.

Continue carefully down the lane and pause at the drive just past number 12 to compare the scene with that of the photograph taken in

Priory Lane in 1972

1972 (Stop I). The cottage is the third timber-framed house reflecting the medieval lay out of *Bovetoun*, although like the other two it probably dates from the 17th century. The cottage in the right foreground of the photograph was typical of those built in the early 19th century although the drip mould above the window appears rather pretentious on such a small cottage. Its demolition allowed the plot to be developed for housing which still largely reflects the planned *Bovetoun* plot of the Later Middle Ages. This was the plot owned by Ann Spencer in 1839, shown as plots 167 and 168 on the Enclosure map.

The ex-Ministry of Works huts of the Old Folk's Association photographed in 1979

Continue along the lane towards School Road. The four large detached houses on the right were part of the Eversfield Gardens development, built on the former pleasure grounds. Yet the first two mask also the existence of the village's senior residents' club which met here from 1959 to 1985 in two huts, brought from a Ministry of Works site in Stoke Road. The club now meets in a purpose-built clubhouse opened in 1988 on the old school site off Pecked Lane, which is fittingly called Denley Hall in commemoration of the family at Eversfield. On the near corner of Fieldgate Road still stands the wall of an old barn – another reminder of the village's farming heritage. Before Fieldgate Road was opened for housing in 1952 it was a quiet country lane, called Velvet or Vulgate Lane, running through orchards full of fruit trees. Twenty four houses were built here as the village continued its post-war expansion. Take care as you make your way to join the route of the main walk in School Road but on your way, where the footpath starts on your left, listen carefully for the noise of the stream which comes down from Woodmancote. It reappears again at Gilder's corner and was the means by which the rector's fishponds were supplied with water in the Middle Ages.

A TOUR AROUND SAINT MICHAEL AND ALL ANGELS CHURCH

THIS TOUR takes you round the outside of the church. When the church is open to visitors you might like to examine the interior using the late Eunice Powell's excellent guide book *Parish Church* from which this plan has been taken.

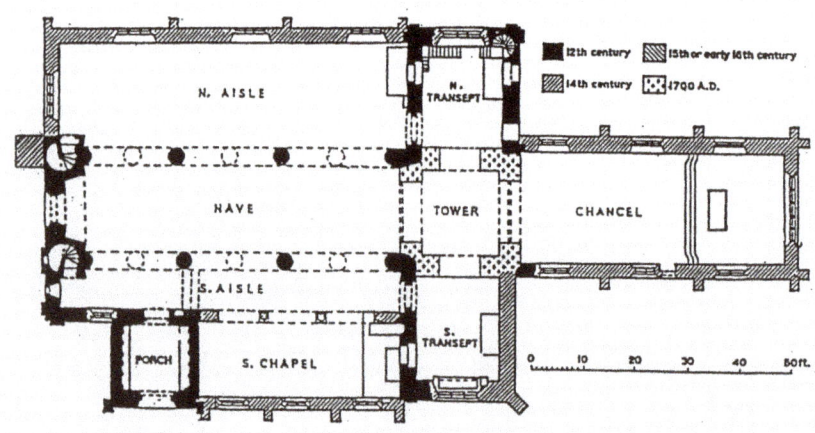

ARCHITECTURAL PERIODS

Norman	c.1066-1160	
Transitional	c.1150-1190	
Early English	c.1190-1250	Gothic
Decorated	c.1250-1350	
Perpendicular	c.1335-1530	

**CHURCH OF ST. MICHAEL AND ALL ANGELS
BISHOP'S CLEEVE**

This church of Saint Michael and All Angels was first recorded towards the end of the 8th century between 777 and 779 and served as the focus for the settlement which became Bishop's Cleeve. It is extremely likely that the present building, originally shaped like a cross, stands on the same spot although its earliest features date only from *c.*1160. This tour starts at the west end and circles the church in an anticlockwise direction.

The West Front

The west front is largely unchanged since the church was built and is a truly imposing feature. Its turrets are more often seen on cathedrals than parish churches and are a sign of the wealth of this church. Take a close look at the doorway. The stonework is typical of the fashionable style of the day – Romanesque, also called Norman because it was mostly introduced into the country after the Norman Conquest in 1066. The Cleeve Hill stone from which it was built is soft and easy to carve when quarried but hardens with age. This has enabled the stonemasons to carve the intricate decorations associated with Romanesque architecture. The arch above the door is a good example of 'Chevron' or 'Dogtooth' design although it has suffered from the effects of the English weather over the centuries. This was a popular design which was taken from Islamic architecture and was used to break up the uniformity and solidness of the stone. Notice the outer ring fleurs de lys which merge into two dragons. The one on the left is baring its teeth; that on the right is eating itself! Dragons seem to have represented the evil ways of the world from which the church protected you. The legend of Saint Michael recounts the slaying of a dragon but dragons are found in many churches, not just those dedicated to Saint Michael.

Now step back from the door to appreciate the other features. The window above the door is of 'Decorated' style and replaced the original, smaller window in the 14th century. Notice how it cuts through the historical string course towards the bottom. Whenever you see a stretch of string course on your way round, you will be looking at the original building. The three very small windows are probably original as is the lower small window at the end of the south aisle on the right. The few surviving fragments of 14th and 15th-century stained glass have been fixed into this window, although they are best seen from the inside. The battlements here and elsewhere are much later, probably 15th century, but the wall still shows the original width of the south aisle. There is a large buttress on your left between the north aisle and the door. This was built in the 14th or 15th century to prevent the collapse of the wall because a spiral staircase had been built inside the turret which weakened its construction. Finally look closely at the graffiti carved into the right-hand column. Keep your eyes open for more graffiti as you move around the church. Now turn the corner and stand in front of the porch.

The Porch

Today the porch is used as the main entrance to the church but in the past it played a much more important rôle. In the Middle Ages baptisms and weddings began in the porch. It was the place where church ale was sold. Right through to the 19th century it was used for secular purposes – signing a business contract and collection of debts. From 1755 the vestry met in the upper room which was also used as a village school. The school seems to have ceased being held there for a while but a schoolmaster called Sperry drew some imaginative scenes on the interior walls in 1818. Both the school and the vestry moved into the National School opposite when it opened in 1847. Forty seven years later the unelected vestry was replaced by an elected parish council. However the porch has not always looked like it does today and historians and

Sperry's tiger on the wall of the school room

This sketch c.1800 shows the graves before they were cleared. The discontinuous string course on the porch has been arrowed

architects have struggled for over 150 years to explain its development. So what follows is but a summary of the latest theories.

Although you can see a stretch of string course, the porch was built slightly later than the body of the church, possibly about 20 years later. One clue is that the string course is not continuous and has a clear stop at its northern end. The chevron moulding above the entrance door is different from that above the west door although it also has a similarity with the two dragon heads which are here very badly weathered. An upper room above this string course was added in the early 14th century when, perhaps, the two buttresses on the porch were also built. Notice how the stone where the string course is missing is yellower than the rest, indicating that the upper room was not extended to the church itself until a century after it had been built, so completing what we see today. To the left of the porch find the Perpendicular window inserted in the south aisle in the 15th century below an original window. Finally before you move on, can you find the three sundials marking the passage of time as the sun moved across the front of the south-facing porch? Two are obvious; the third less so.

The South Aisle

The south aisle was widened c.1320 to fill the space between the porch and the south transept which, together with the north transept, formed the arms of the cross of the original plan. By comparing the width of the south aisle here with what you have already seen on the other side of the porch, you can see how much it was enlarged. The late Perpendicular style of the windows indicate they were inserted over a century later but the stained glass in them only dates from the turn of the 20th century.

The south aisle seems to have been built as a chantry chapel with its own altar where a priest would say daily prayers for the souls of the dead. He might also teach the children and it is not impossible the upper room in the porch was built as his accommodation. His was a separate responsibility from the rector's; his income coming from bequests from wealthy villagers who left money in their wills for a priest to pray for their souls. In 1419 the rector Richard Reve left money for a chaplain to pray for ten years. In 1542 William Hobby left £4.13s.4d (£4.66p or approximately £4000 today) for 'an honest priest' to sing for his own and his parents' souls for a year. He left each son £4! Such chantries were ended by an Act of Parliament in 1547. The aisle then became known as the Southam side until 1862, when Lord Ellenborough restored the ruined medieval chapel at Southam for worship.

Gargoyles and grotesques

Before moving on, look up at the weathered remains of gargoyles, decorative waterspouts often in the shape of dragons which again represented the evil kept outside by what took place inside the church. Look out for them as you walk around. Now move on to the south transept and study the grotesques, the small carved heads at the foot of the window arches. Some seem to represent individuals, but others are animals – the monkey and the sheep representing the foolishness of humans. Both gargoyles and grotesques spoke to illiterate people about the protective power of the church in the later Middle Ages.

A gargoyle and a grotesque

The South Transept
This was extensively rebuilt in the 14th century but two original string courses still survive to the left of the Decorated window. The grotesques can be followed round to the north transept which would suggest that both transepts were modified when the chancel was built.

The Chancel
The upkeep of the nave was the responsibility of the villagers but the chancel with its altar was the responsibility of the rector. The rector from 1273 to 1284 was Walter Scammell. He was also dean of Salisbury Cathedral until 1284, when he became the Bishop of Salisbury and so relinquished the rectory of Bishop's Cleeve. However, he left £40 to build an enlarged chancel and repair houses on the rector's manor. We know this because the record tells us that nothing had happened by 1301. From the style of the windows the construction must have started shortly after that date. The five hundred roofing slates brought from Ash quarry on Cleeve Hill in 1389-90 might have been to complete the roof or for repairing it. Externally the chancel remains almost unchanged except the stained glass in its windows has long since been destroyed. The varied colour of the stone used in the walls indicates that it had been obtained from a number of different quarries on Cleeve Hill. The Decorated windows, the priest's door with its eroding ball flowers and the 'pellet work' below the gutters are good examples of early 14th-century architecture. However there are three windows which need further consideration. Look at the carving at the top of the window

nearest the transept. It is quite crude and lacks the finesse of similar windows. This is a puzzle for which the usual explanation is that it was an attempt to copy the original which was destroyed when the spire fell down in 1696. However, the surrounding stonework looks original with no signs of a join, which tends to throw doubt on the explanation, but doesn't provide an alternative. The third window is the impressive east window which is a replica. In the late 19th century the building was very neglected and needed urgent restoration. When H.E. Branch visited St Michael's in 1886 as he prepared to write his book *Cotswold and Vale* (1904) he commented that the church displayed "a spectacle of desolation and dust of fallen plaster and mouldering timber". Renovations started in 1891 and cost £4170, of which £230 was still owed to the builders in 1908, although the church had been reopened in 1900. These renovations included the replica east window set within the original arch.

Move on past this window to the north side of the church. Suddenly the atmosphere changes and even on a warm summer's day it can feel gloomy and remote. Here on the north side the limewash which covered the walls of the church, until most of it was removed in 1894 during the renovations, is best preserved. Earlier records give several references to the campaigns of limewashing. In 1815 it cost £37.6s.8d. (£37.33p) with an extra 1s.6d. (7½p) to clear up the mess!

An example of graffiti on an existing patch of limewash

The North Transept

The side of the north transept which faces you tells yet another story. The string course and window remain from the original building. So too does the blocked doorway. Once this led outside into the graveyard but the enlarging of the chancel made it useless and it was blocked up. The scar of a roof which ends at the window is a mystery as there is no other evidence for a building here. As in the south aisle, a new enlarged window was created on the north side destroying the original window; all part of the rebuilding of the church which took place in the first half of the 14th century.

The North Aisle
The theme of extensive building in the 14th century continues as this is the date of the north aisle, probably built in the middle years of that century. The windows are original but the stained glass in them dates only from the early 20th century. Why was this aisle built? Perhaps a clue lies in its historical name - the Gotherington aisle. In the Later Middle Ages the people of Gotherington came to St Michael's for baptisms, burials and funerals. In fact the footpath which links the churchyard to Station Road is the last part of a footpath, commonly called the coffin path, which can be followed even through the modern housing estates to Shutter Lane in Gotherington, where there is a sign 'Church Walk' and 'Coffin Path', confirming the link to St Michael's. In 1545 John Kemmett of Gotherington left 20d (8p) to mend the way 'as men goeth to the church between Gotherington and Cleeve'. There did exist a small chapel for regular worshipping in Gotherington but it was said to be derelict by the early 14th century. It might be that the north aisle was built about this time to cater for the villagers who had worshipped at that chapel. As you leave the north aisle notice on the corner the largest surviving area of limewash.

The West Front again
We have now returned to our starting point but as you turn the corner towards the west front look up at the two grotesques at the end of the north aisle. Both are very unusual and mysterious; the one has a man who is holding open the mouth of a small creature between his legs. The other has a man holding what appears to be the head of a dog under his right arm although there is no recognisable body attached. People have tried to guess their meaning but they still remain a mystery.

The Tower
Stand at a distance from the porch to have a good view of the tower. It seems to sit naturally above the rest of the church, but this masks a confusing history. One historian has suggested the chancel had to be

rebuilt in the early 14th century because an earlier tower collapsed into it. As early as 1563 concern was expressed over the poor condition of the church. In 1635 an inspection by the Bishop of Gloucester's surveyors found that the steeple and bells were in a state of decay and the rector Timothy Gates was ordered to take action before the next visitation. Whatever Timothy did was not successful because in 1696 the spire collapsed, 'for want of timely reparation' wrote historian Abel Wantner in 1700. He continued 'which was rebuilt as now (i.e. 1700) and standeth without a steeple… which cost above £570'. We also know that in 1696 the churchwardens paid the architect James Hill of Cheltenham sixteen shillings (80p) for a draft plan for the tower and the final bill was around £770. Historians have since argued how much of the existing tower had to be rebuilt. Inside the church the columns which support the tower date from that period but we don't know how much of the tower above had to be rebuilt. It does look like a tower built in the 15th century with its Perpendicular window openings and gargoyles, but is it just a copy of the original? The pinnacles and gargoyles on top of the tower are in the style contemporary with the time of the rebuild. The narrow windows at the bottom of the tower could survive from an earlier original tower or they could be copies. There are no obvious clues inside the tower, either, although we

The style of gargoyle on the tower suggests it was mostly rebuilt after the steeple collapsed in 1696

know a new great bell was purchased in 1715 at a cost of £15, suggesting it was not only the spire which collapsed. So, we will probably never know the exact story. However, we do know about the clock which dates from the renovations in 1894 and cost £138.10s. (£138.50p) and also the weathervane which was erected in 1966 showing Saint Michael triumphing over a dragon. One final feature to notice before you move on is the dormer window inserted in the roof of the nave during the late 19th-century restoration to allow more light into the interior.

The Churchyard

The history of the last 300 years could be traced in the tombstones in the churchyard even though many have been removed in recent years, but take care if you want to walk around them. The most impressive is the table tomb to the Barnes family which stands on its own. It dates from 1749 and is a protected listed building. The Barnes family ran one of the watermills in Stockwell Lane in Woodmancote and continues to be one of the oldest established local families.

Look round the edges of the churchyard. You can see the close relationship between the National School and its sponsoring church. Standing between Church Road and the entrance to the churchyard, the rectory of 1972 is much closer to the church than the earlier rectory at the former bishop's manor house, but not as close as The Priory, the earliest rectory. Also notice how Gothic Cottage fronts onto a long-disused entry into the churchyard. Finally, as you retrace your steps to the entrance, find on the left the only First World War Imperial War Gravestone in the graveyard – to Donald Page who died in Hilsea military hospital in Portsmouth in 1916. Donald was one of the 21 fallen of the Great War whose names appear on the war memorial who actually lived in Bishop's Cleeve and Woodmancote.

This is one of two Second World War Commonwealth War Graves in the churchyard. Can you find the other one?

CASE STUDY 1
OLDACRE'S

ALTHOUGH THE MILL has completely disappeared and Tesco supermarket and car park were laid out on its site, leaving only its office block and show room still standing on Church Road, the story of Oldacre's is an important part of the history of the village because the business had an influence as its largest single employer and showed how a large enterprise could grow out of a small village. Not only that, but its influence extended far beyond the local area. Walter John Oldacre, born in 1862, was a young man with ambition. By the time he was twenty he was operating as a country carrier taking local people and produce to Cheltenham three times a week and carrying out errands for those unable to go. The expansion of his business really began in 1881 when he moved to lodge at what is now Owl's End House, 87 Station Road,

Owl's End House, then called St Margaret's. Are the people Maria and Lucy Minett?

then called St Margaret's. Walter John knew the owners, the Minett family very well as it used his carrier's business to take their vegetables, butter, cheese, fruit and cider to sell in Cheltenham. Henry Minett's cider-making was based in a number of outbuildings and when he died in January 1881 Walter saw the potential of using them for his business. That was one reason he moved in to lodge with Henry's widow Maria and daughter Lucy. The same year he bought his first rick of hay for £35 to truss and sell on. From there he moved to buying animal foodstuffs in bulk and retailing them. By 1885 he had the first steam engine in the village in one of the outbuildings where he ground his own feeds and that of local farmers. By this time he had also married Lucy, Henry's daughter, and he had begun to rent land around the village to grow his own hay for sale. In 1890 he bought The Pollards, which stood near the

The Pollards in Church Road in 1976, the year before it was demolished

junction of Cheltenham Road and Church Road, with nearly 5a (2ha) of land extending behind the Tithe Barn. It was here he developed his business which grew to be the largest in the village. Ten years later he was renting Dean Farm to the north west of the village to grow his own hay for selling. In 1907 he opened a shop in Winchcombe Street in Cheltenham.

The firm W.J. Oldacre Ltd was founded in 1923 by which time Walter John was importing maize from the USA via Bishop's Cleeve railway station. He now had a transport fleet of ten wagons, twenty five horses and even four railway wagons. In 1926 he went to live in Fieldgate Farm in Pecked Lane, a short distance from the mill and the village centre. The next year he took on land at Withy Furlong Farm in Stoke Road, and three years later took over Walker's bakery and corn business in Charlton Kings. Even though the mill in Bishop's Cleeve suffered a devastating fire in 1931, the business continued to expand and a new mill was built. As he grew older, he passed more on to his son William John, and the expansion continued after the death of Walter John in 1933. A demonstration pig unit containing six hundred pigs was set up at Linworth Farm in 1935; houses for the Smiths' estate were built on that land in the early 1950s. The name is commemorated by Linworth Road and the farm itself stood on Two Hedges Road opposite what is now Cleeve School. From here thirty pigs per week were sent to Birmingham. In 1937 a shop and warehouse in Tewkesbury were added to the business, and by 1938 the company had invested in modern transport with three lorries, soon to be followed by tractors for the farming. This in turn led to the setting up of a garage, primarily at first

Oldacre's mill

to service the vehicles, but it soon began to sell petrol to motorists. By the outbreak of war Oldacre's had become a modern firm situated in a traditional village. It had done well in the difficult inter-war years through innovation, careful management and firm family control as it responded to the commercial market. At the outbreak of the Second World War the firm was Bishop's Cleeve's biggest single employer, with over thirty people working at its Church Road headquarters.

It was an integrated business with interests in farmland, crops and animals to the retailing of seed, foodstuffs and even bread and cakes. Its land stretched from Stoke Road towards Woodmancote and with the purchase of Cleevelands Farm in Station Road in 1942 and Yew Tree Farm in Gotherington in 1950, the company owned practically all the land between the two villages. In 1958 Homelands Farm was built between the two villages as the land of Cleevelands Farm was sold for building. More recently, in 1996 Wimpey bought Homelands Farm which extended to 304a (127ha) for £1.3m to build 1800 houses as the village continued to expand.

Oldacre's continued to expand in the post-war world and not just by acquiring land. It diversified into intensive beef rearing and fat lamb production. In 1953 it bought out W. Ride and Company, seed merchants in Cheltenham; in 1969 it opened a new feed mill in Calne in Wiltshire, at which time it had over one hundred employees. In May 1975 it moved into the former Bishop of Worcester's manor house as its headquarters - a visible sign of self-confidence. Oldacre's had become the largest animal feed processing company in private ownership. In December 1978 it opened a car showroom in School

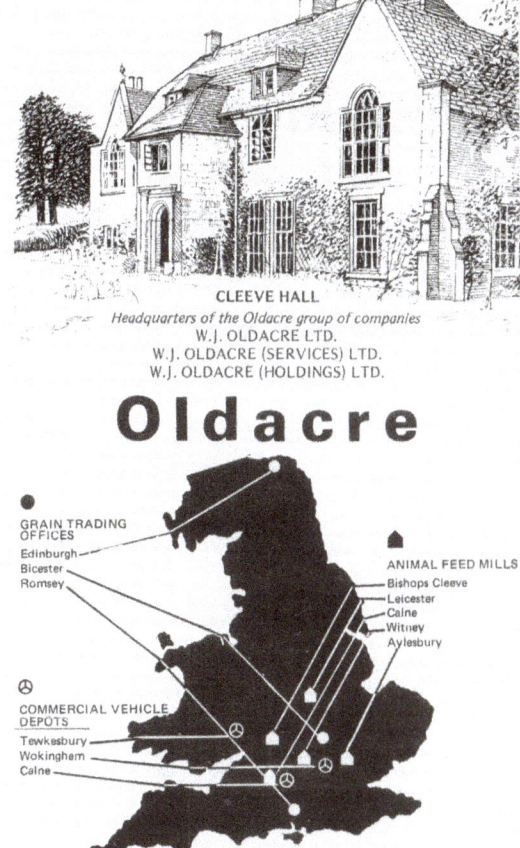

Oldacre's extensive interests in 1977

Oldacre's site shortly after closure

Road (now Cat's Whiskers), as it became a multi-million pound business with diverse interests. It became a public company in 1984, but in 1985 the European Community introduced quotas on milk production, which directly affected the market for animal food. At about the same time food surpluses began to build up in Europe. Although the company was still profitable, it made the directors think, and a good offer from Unigate of £26 million in August 1986 saw this important local company sold out of local hands. Seven years later, Unigate sold it to Dalgety for £23 million. As part of a much larger company, it was now subject to decisions taken far away from Bishop's Cleeve, and in May 1996 the mill was closed. It had been a significant feature of the village for just over a century but it then became part of its history and released a site for the building of the Tesco supermarket. Denys Charnock's book *Oldacre: A Gloucestershire Family and Business* contains a detailed account of the history of the firm. See *Further Reading* for the details.

CASE STUDY 2
CLEEVE HALL

This is without doubt the most prestigious domestic building in the village; built as a manor house for the Bishop of Worcester, who acquired the manor in the early 9th century. Yet the history of the site goes back much further. Archaeological excavations, carried out in 1998 when Bovis Homes was building an extension at the back, discovered Romano-British ditches containing 2nd to 4th-century pottery and also evidence for the high status Roman villa which has not yet been located. Further investigations showed that the present building's immediate forerunner was a large Anglo-Saxon timber-framed hall. It must have been in this hall in the last quarter of the 11th century that Bishop Wulfstan performed three miraculous cures, including the curing of a

'madman', which people interpreted as imitating Jesus' action recorded in chapter five of Mark's gospel.

The building which exists today was started by Bishop Godfrey Giffard (1268–1302). This would fit into Bishop Giffard's known achievements to increase the land held by the bishopric and carry out a building programme which included additions to his manor house at Hartlebury and his palace in Worcester. At the same time he was concerned his income was not keeping up with expenditure and in 1286 he tried to take over the rector's manor for extra income. His appeal to the Pope in Rome was not successful as he was only allowed to take it over during his life time but not as a permanent acquisition. He complained he had spent £200 (approximately £¼m today) on the case. The central part of that house was the hall, which was open to the roof. The north wing was built at right angles to contain the private quarters, and the south wing containing the buttery (for drink) and pantry (for food) was at first parallel to the road but then was extended at the front in the late 15th or early 16th century so that it matched the north wing. We are not sure whether the kitchen was in the south wing or originally detached so that if it caught fire from its open fires, only the kitchen and not the house itself, would have been destroyed. The servants would have lived in the south wing. A detailed building survey carried out in 2001 declared that the timbers of the north wing, with their twenty four pairs of coupled rafters lacking purlins to link them together, are among the finest of their type in the country. The date of 1667 on the porch, by which time the building had become the rectory, marks major alterations by the then rector, William Nicholson, who was also the Bishop of Gloucester. The walls were raised to two and a half storeys, the front made flush with the wings and a new porch was added. A projecting staircase at the rear is not visible from the road. Samuel Pickering (rector 1770–1815) introduced the Venetian windows and so, apart from the demolition of the rear of the south wing in 1920, that is the building we see from the road today. But what a story its walls could tell!

We must not think of it as the permanent home of the Bishop of Worcester, for he had a palace in Worcester and a dozen other residences including at Alvechurch, Kempsey and Hartlebury as well as here in Bishop's Cleeve. The bishops' registers recorded when they actually visited, often on their way to their manor at Westbury on Trym near

Bristol; for example on 19 September 1320 Bishop Thomas Cobham ordained three priests in the chapel on the ground floor of the north wing. In 1328 Bishop Adam de Orleton stayed for two weeks. In 1335 Bishop Simon de Montacute stopped on his way between his manors of Bredon and Withington and preached a sermon in St Michael's. The bishops moved with a large entourage which needed accommodation and feeding from the produce of the manor. Yet there were bishops who we know never visited at all; between 1499 and 1535 two bishops were Italians living in Italy. However, apart from visits by the bishop and by his steward, the building must have lain empty. The steward was responsible for the smooth running of the manor, ensuring the tenants fulfilled their obligations, which included working on the bishop's demesne as part payment for their holdings. There they grew mostly barley and oats in the 13th and 14th centuries, with some wheat to sell for cash to make their cash payments to the bishop in addition to their labour services. Only in the 15th century did they begin to grow wheat for flour for their own consumption. A few tenants were freeholders who only paid a money rent but by 1426 nearly everybody was only paying rent, which released them from their labour services and allowed them to spend more time on their own land and working for wages on the land of those tenants with large land holdings. The rents ensured the bishop had a steady income. The bishop's demesne was large; in 1400 it was recorded as 400a (167ha). The produce was used to supply the bishop and his household and the surplus was sold. Further income came from the sale of wool. In the summer of 1299 a thousand of the bishop's sheep were recorded grazing on the common on Cleeve Hill. In 1394 the flock was 400 but with a combined total together with the villagers' sheep of 3000, Cleeve Common must have looked a very busy place, as sheep were not the only farm animals put to graze there.

In 1400 the bishop's income from all his manors, which were mostly scattered across the West Midlands, was £1200 (almost £1million in today's values). The size of the Tithe Barn indicates the large amount of grain produced on the bishop's demesne. The records tell us that it stood in a farmyard with a granary, a kiln for drying grain, hayricks, pigsties and a sheepcote, all now demolished, the pig sties being the last to go in 1890. By the house itself were found the stables and dovecote, both now converted into dwellings. As the Reformation developed during the middle of the 16th century, in 1561 the bishop's manor came into the hands of Queen Elizabeth I. It then passed through the hands of several holders until in 1624 the house, buildings and 486a (202ha) of land were bought by Timothy Gates, the rector of Bishop's Cleeve for £3000. This was a huge sum when farm labourers were earning £5 a year. Timothy moved out of the original rectory, now The Priory in Station Road, to make a home for his family of five children in addition to three children from his wife Catharine's first marriage. With their servants the newly-acquired rectory must have hummed with activity. It would take a whole book to cover all its subsequent history and so here are just a few highlights.

Until the beginning of the 20th century Bishop's Cleeve's rectory was one of the richest livings in England. It had extensive glebe land, which extended to over 100a (42ha) with six cottages and seven other rented properties in 1589, and which was still being referred to as a manor in 1735. By 1914 the glebe had grown to 450a (188ha) and provided an income of £700 (approximately £80,000 today) largely through the creation of Gotherington Fields Farm (280a [117ha]) as compensation for lost tithes as a result of the enclosure of Gotherington in 1807 and Glebe Farm (118a [50ha]) along Stoke Road, created for the same reason in Bishop's Cleeve in 1847. In addition to the income from these farms, the tithes themselves were converted into money payments in 1839, which continued until 1936. They were worth £1470 a year in 1839 (approximately £150,000 today). So from 1624 to 1839 the barn which had belonged to the Bishop of Worcester could now be correctly called a tithe barn for storing the produce of the rector's lands and that name has persisted until the present day.

The records tell us that at least from the Later Middle Ages, the wealth of the rectory seems to have attracted clergy who were already well off and hardly, if ever, visited the village (see *Case Study 4* for more on this). Many of them took the income and paid a preacher or a curate to care for the villagers' souls. Timothy Gate's wife was Catherine Bridges, the granddaughter of Sir John Bridges, the first Lord Chandos of Sudeley and a wealthy man. Timothy himself owned land and was also an entrepreneur who was a partner in the tobacco growing venture based on Winchcombe in 1619. In 1623 he was recorded as the only person living in the village belonging to the gentry. The yearly income for the rectory alone was £500 (approximately £100,000 today) in 1650, no doubt largely enjoyed by Timothy who was paying Thomas Wynell to conduct the preaching. For a short period Timothy could have been regarded as a 'squarson' – the lord of the manor who was also the parson, but in 1659 he sold all the land of the former bishop's manor except the house and land immediately around it. He died in 1661. Thomas Wynell, like the other preachers and curates who did the church's interacting with the villagers, would also have carried out the such duties as baptising, marrying and burying the parishioners for which he would have received additional fees. For more on the descent of the former bishop's manor, see *Case Study 5*.

The rectors who followed Timothy did not necessarily live in the rectory house. William Nicholson was appointed Bishop of Gloucester in 1661. Notwithstanding he was also archdeacon of Brecon and a canon of St David's Cathedral he became rector of Bishop's Cleeve in 1665 to increase his income as a bishop. He obviously took an interest in the village because he enlarged the rectory and put his initials above the porch. He died in 1672. James Uvedale became rector in 1709 and within two years asked for permission to demolish the whole of the north wing which he claimed was in a poor condition, could not be used and would cost £100 to repair. Fortunately permission was refused and the so Cleeve Hall continues to present an almost symmetrical appearance to the passer-by.

Affluent rectors continued to be appointed into the 19th century. Some lived in the rectory, others continued to live elsewhere but they all employed at least one curate for their day to day obligations, especially conducting the Sunday and holy day services. Samuel Pickering, who added the Venetian windows, appointed three curates at different times and left £4700 (approximately £425,000 today) in ready money in his will. Robert Lawrence Townsend, who followed him, owned an estate at Steanbridge near Stroud before becoming rector and he left £6000 in ready money on his death in 1830. His annual income from the rectory was recorded as £1400 in 1815 when a labourer might have earned £15 a year. A wonderful mural survives upstairs in Cleeve Hall which records life in Steanbridge before he moved to Bishop's Cleeve. Robert paid his son William £100 a year to serve as his curate but when Robert died in 1830, William followed him as rector until his death in

1883. In 1830 he was also granted the rectory of Alderton, annual value of £450, by which time the annual value of Bishop's Cleeve was estimated at £1700 (approximately £200,000 today). However, he lived away for much of the time, ostensibly as a result of ill-health. In the 1861 census he was recorded with his wife and one servant living in Brighton. This enabled some of his curates to live in the rectory, but like his father he paid them £100 a year.

The mural extends around the room (Vistry Cotswolds)

On census night in March 1851 Henry Palmer (curate 1845–51) was living there with his wife Louise and their two children, plus a butler, cook and three other servants. How could a curate on £100 a year afford such a household? The clue lies in his place of birth, recorded as Jamaica. In 1821 his father had sold three coffee growing estates for £40,000 (approximately £4.4m today). Henry had siblings so we don't know his share of the inheritance, but when he died in 1873 his estate was valued at £20,000 (perhaps £2.3m today). With such sums derived from West Indian slavery it was no wonder Henry could afford a large household. Henry was the clergyman who was taking the services in St Michael's on census Sunday in March 1851 when attendances at all services in all the country's places of worship were counted; a survey which has never been

A close up, possibly showing Robert Townsend and his bride at Steanbridge (Vistry Cotswolds)

repeated. The morning attendance was 143 and the afternoon's 201. Henry added that there was bad weather perhaps indicating the figures were lower than usual. Unfortunately we don't know how many people attended both services and were counted twice and we don't know how many came from Gotherington, Southam and Woodmancote, which all lacked an Anglican place of worship. However the total attendances represented about forty per cent of the village's population.

Henry left the village later that year and moved to live in Cheltenham. Like many of the curates he did not stay long, but unlike Benjamin Hemming who became the senior curate in 1873. In 1881 he was living in the rectory with his wife Katherine, eight year old daughter Mabel together with a nurse, cook, housemaid, parlour maid and groom. No other family in the village enjoyed such a household and so it is no surprise when, two years later, Benjamin became the rector and occupied

Benjamin Hemming on the rectory lake, where Pullar Court now stands

the rectory in his own right for the next twelve years. Benjamin had been born in Honeybourne in Worcestershire but unlike Henry Palmer, I have not been able to discover the origins of his personal wealth. This pattern of affluent background continued into the 20th century. Thomas Jesson (rector 1895-1919) came from West Bromwich where his family had made their fortune as ironmongers, buying a small estate which Thomas gave to the borough with its house in 1912 and out of which was created Jesson Park in 1955. His son also served as rector from 1932 to 1947.

The line of affluent rectors continued into the 20th century but the equalisation of the clergy's income across the Church of England, loss of income from tithes and the decreasing size of the glebe, only 30a (12ha) in 1964 and 10a (4ha) in 2019, together with increasing secularisation, the decline of church influence in daily life and the costs of maintaining the large medieval building lacking modern comforts were factors which led to the rector leaving the historic building in 1972. This was then sold to Oldacre's in 1974 as their prestigious headquarters, who gave it the present name of Cleeve Hall. A much more manageable and comfortable house was built as a modern rectory by the entrance to the churchyard. With the closure of Oldacre's in 1996, Bovis Homes (now part of the Vistry group) purchased it for their regional headquarters and enlarging their offices at the rear left the historic front unchanged. Cleeve Hall, the former Bishop of Worcester's manor house and then rectory, continues to dominate this part of the village.

Kenneth Edmunds with his wife Mary and their family was the last rector to live in Cleeve Hall. The couple are seen here with the Bishop of Tewkesbury, Robert Deakin

left: This view of Cleeve Hall, probably taken in the 1950s, shows the kitchen garden with the dovecot and, on the left hand side of the picture, the stables

CASE STUDY 3
CLEEVEWAY MANOR

A**LTHOUGH NOT** one of the oldest houses in the village, the history of Cleeveway Manor contains some interesting episodes which are worth recounting to provide a glimpse into some of the main social trends affecting the village in the last two hundred years. The house itself seems to have originated before the 18th century but the building as it now stands was enlarged during the 19th century at right angles to the original building, to create one of the largest prestigious domestic buildings in the village. For much of its recorded history it was known as Cleeve House, but also The Cleevelands and The Cleeveway before it took on its present name as Cleeveway Manor. It was never a manor like those of the bishop and rector, as its origins were as a farmstead.

The earliest reference I have found dates from 1739 when the Hyett family had owned a farm called Bates' Place for many years. We

The Cleeveway c.1840

have a description of the site in 1814. This included the farm house, barns, stables, a mill house (presumably to grind corn) and a dovecot with unspecified other buildings, fold yards (for animals) and other yards, gardens with an adjoining orchard. The whole was owned and occupied by William Taylor who owned further land scattered around the village, including the elongated plot of land between Priory Lane and Station Road, on part of which Eversfield House stands but the accompanying tea gardens have long since disappeared (See *Case Study 6*). The archives then become rather confusing for there exists a sale record of William Taylor's estate in 1841 by which time William had died and the estate was in the hands of his trustees. It was described as a house with garden, barn, stables, outbuildings, fold yard and rickyard (for hay and fodder). However the Tithe map of 1839 recorded it as being owned by Sarah Griffiths, the widow of a Cheltenham solicitor Thomas Griffiths. The farm was large, 71a (30ha) in extent, with the lands spread right across the village fields. It was an investment for Sarah who must have valued the rent paid by the farmer Richard Rayer who lived in The Cleevelands and rented 9a (4ha) of her land. All the rest of her land was rented to Thomas Hobbs who both owned and rented 136a (45ha) from his farmstead in Stockwell Lane in Woodmancote. By 1847 when the village's remaining open fields had been enclosed and divided it into hedged fields, a process which had taken nine years, we can see from the map accompanying the enclosure award that her land was spread all around the village. In addition to the land which immediately surrounded the farmstead, Sarah owned fields bordering Two Hedges Road in the south to fields between Meadoway and Stoke Road including where Grangefield school and the Capita building now stand, to fields in the north including where the Cleevelands estate roundabout has been built. However, all this land was rented out to enable her to enjoy the income and so it is no surprise that in the 1851 census we find her, aged 60, living in Cheltenham as a widowed landed proprietor with two servants.

The same census informs us that the house in Bishop's Cleeve was the home of Septimus Pruen, his wife Louisa and one-year-old son George and three servants. Septimus is the first of a number of interesting people who can be traced living in this house. He was a solicitor in Cheltenham, author of the town's Improvement Act of 1852 and partner in the law firm of Pruen and Griffiths. The family could only have lived there for a relatively short time because in 1858 we find them living at 30 Cambray Place in Cheltenham. But how did they come to be living in Bishop's Cleeve?

A deed of 1832 indicates that an Edward Pruen had a financial interest in the estate, as did the Griffiths family. Then there was a close family connection, for Louisa Pruen was Sarah's Griffiths daughter. Living with them, but identified in the census as living in a separate household in the same building, was Louisa's brother Frederick Thomas, also a solicitor who later became the deputy clerk to the County Court in Cheltenham. We can imagine Septimus and Frederick on their daily journey with the pony and trap struggling up Park Bank on the way to the town. This episode in the story of The Cleevelands is worth rescuing from history for as far as I have discovered Septimus was the original commuter out of the village, setting a trend today followed by thousands who choose to live in the village but work elsewhere. Although his fellow villagers, the agricultural labourers, also travelled to work, they travelled on foot to the surrounding villages and did not always travel to the same place, unlike Septimus.

After Sarah's death, in 1865 Frederick Griffiths sold The Cleevelands to George Stephenson for £2000. No doubt this enabled him to build The Grange. At the sale it was no longer described as a farm house, but a mansion house, by which time it must have taken on its present appearance. George was still there in 1868 and the Stephensons continued to own the property although by 1885 they were renting it out. There is an intriguing entry in Kelly's Directory for 1889 which states that Mrs Stephenson had turned it into a convalescent home for children from London hospitals. Mrs Stephenson, George's widow, was a local philanthropist who at the time was recorded as living at Southfield in Station Road. I have come to the conclusion that the intention to turn it into a children's home never happened because in 1891 Thomas Mace, his wife Catherine, father-in-law James Burns, baby Mary and Mary's nurse Lizzie Salisbury were living there. Thomas gave his occupation as a farmer. In 1895 The Cleevelands was put up for sale as farm of 70a (29ha) but at the time of the census of 1901 it was home to William East, his wife Mary and three daughters for whom they employed a governess with a further six servants. William did not work for a living, being a retired Bombay civil servant. By then, Sarah Griffiths' extensive landholding had been dispersed. On her land between Meadoway and Stoke Road her solicitor son Frederick had built The Grange in 1866. Frederick employed a bailiff to run his mixed farm of 90 acres (38 ha), which gave him time to work as a solicitor in Cheltenham and involve himself in village affairs. The farm buildings stood on Cheltenham Road near the present traffic lights but only the

The Grange in 1988

house still stands. In 1939 Smiths Industries bought The Grange for £7000 moving from London as the first step to set up the factory which today belongs to GE Aviation, whose parent organisation is found in Ohio USA. The loss of land and the relocation of the farm to The Grange by 1901 meant that The Cleevelands had become just a prestigious mansion on the edge of the village.

In 1906 it was the home of Colonel Alfred Barnett DSO. Five years later its status as a country mansion was very probably the reason it had become home to another army officer, Walter Lascelles and his wife Louisa with their servants, a footman, cook, lady's maid, house maid and kitchen maid. Walter was the grandson of the third Earl of Harewood and a cousin to Mrs Dent-Brocklehurst of Sudeley Castle. He had had a distinguished career in the Durham Light Infantry, having been mentioned in dispatches during the Boer War in South Africa where he had been badly wounded. After the war he had married Louisa in 1902 and they were subsequently frequent visitors to Cheltenham, which might have been a factor in the decision to purchase Cleeve House, as it was now called, probably in 1909. Walter was rich and only the second person in the village to own a car, a 15hp Austin tourer which he bought in September 1910. Coincidentally the first person to own a car in the village was living at The Grange – James McClymont Reid had purchased a 48hp Daimler exactly a year earlier and as a friend of Walter he might just have given him the idea. In the 1911 census James is recorded as the 50-year-old managing director of the Argentina Land Company. He, his wife Caroline and two daughters had all been born in Argentina. It was obviously a very profitable position as they employed ten servants. They provide another excellent example of how Bishop's Cleeve was beginning to attract affluent

Walter Lascelles' memorial window in St Michael's church

inhabitants who did not have a need to live here for their work.

The census in 1911 was taken on Sunday, 2 April. On Thursday 18 May Walter died peacefully at home, aged only 44; perhaps his old army wounds were a factor. He left £16,751 (approximately £2m today) which enabled his wife Louisa to lead the life of a leisured lady, but she did not let the grass grow under her feet after her husband's death. She attempted to take on the rôle of lady of the manor - a traditional rôle which has never existed in the village. In March 1928 she was elected unopposed to represent the village on Winchcombe Rural District Council, but she did not continue when Cheltenham Rural District Council replaced that of Winchcombe in 1935. She was one of the first two ladies ever to be elected to the council. Older villagers still remember her as a popular figure around the village. She died in a nursing home in Cheltenham in June 1954.

Taking tea at a Conservative Party gathering at The Cleeveway c.1950. W.S. Morrison was the local MP for thirty years from 1929-1959 and served as speaker of the House of Commons for the last eight. He is speaking to Mrs G. Ward, who was the village's county councillor for twenty years, and Mrs Bowsher. Mrs Ward's daughter Susannah seems more interested in the photograph being taken

Louisa supported the Conservative party as did the Bowshers who followed her at The Cleevelands. Reginald Bowsher was conductor of the village choral society. In December 1946 he wrote an interesting letter to the *Gloucestershire Echo* explaining how three German prisoners of war, deputed to remove decaying wartime Nissen huts from his land, spent all day sitting around a fire, drinking tea and playing cards. He called this "Disgraceful" and concluded his letter "I wonder what the position would have been if Germany had won the war?" After the Bowshers the house became a renowned hotel and restaurant before returning to be the private residence it is today.

CASE STUDY 4
THE PRIORY

THE PRIORY is now hidden away from public view but it stands with Cleeve Hall as the two most significant domestic buildings in the village's history. When the Bishop of Worcester acquired the territory which had been the royal estate which had been granted for the upkeep of a *monasterium aet Clife*, a portion of that estate was reserved to support the church. A priest was recorded in the Domesday Book of

The Priory in 1964 with Cleevelands Farm in the middle distance

1087. Thus began one of the richest church livings in the county until the Anglican church re-organised its finances in the 20th century. It is not unreasonable to suggest that the whole of the area bounded by the roads in this walk originally belonged to the rectory and this was a significant reason why the Bishop of Worcester had to build his manor house away from the area around the church. The geographical position of The Priory and the references to it in the archives confirm that it was the rectory until 1624. The following summary of the key people, events and circumstances in the history of The Priory is rather like trying to complete a jigsaw puzzle with many of the pieces missing, but despite this it is worth the attempt.

We can start by considering the relative size of the rector's manor compared to the bishop's. Our earliest detailed reference comes from the Later Middle Ages when in the tax list of 1327 the rector's tenants are listed separately from those of the bishop and were ten in number, paying a collective tax of 12s.5d. (63p); the bishop had twenty four tenants, paying 61s.1½d. (£3.6p). Although we don't know how many were exempt from paying the tax, it was obviously not as large as the bishop's manor and the individuals were not as wealthy, based on the individual taxes paid, but it was still a significant part of the village. In particular the much changed area around the war memorial down to the two large shops in Tobyfield Road was called 'Cheapside'. This is where the village's shops were located in the Later Middle Ages and they all belonged to the rector. There were also other tenants who held their cottages and farms from the rector and worked on his demesne to pay part of their rent. We are extremely fortunate that Corpus Christi College Oxford holds rectory records from 1389 to 1418. They show the wealth of the rector. In 1389 his annual income was £96 from the produce of his lands and tithes. In that year alone the tithes he received included 134 lambs, 37 piglets, 113 doves, 30 geese, 1080 eggs and wool from 3000 sheep. His tenants collectively had to work a total 824 days each year on his demesne. The fees he received from the duties of a parish priest, leading services on Sundays and Holy Days (of which there were over 40 each year), baptising, marrying and burying, were in addition but usually granted to a curate who performed them. To give some idea of his wealth, the slatter who was working on the roof of the chancel of St Michael's church in the same year was paid 3d (1¼p) a day and the women who prepared the thatch, possibly to re-roof four of the rector's shops in Cheapside in 1417, received 2d (1p) a day.

We have noted that ten tenants were recorded in 1327; in 1463 thirteen tenants were renting 87a (36ha) between them and in 1589 we learn the rector owned thirteen dwellings. By this latter date the land attached to the rectory was recorded as the glebe. It extended to 91a (38ha) and was rented out to William Potter so that the rector received a money payment instead of having to organise its cultivation. The process of leasing out the glebe for a fee can be traced back to 1418 at least. It meant the lessee, also known as the farmer, took all the risks and the rector was assured of an income, although by that time the tenants were themselves paying rents rather than carrying out labour services. Most, if not all, the tenants seem originally to have been cotlanders or mondaymen and as the population fell from the early 14th century and then the Black Death of 1348-49, enterprising tenants increased their holdings; in 1479 John Hiatt held a messuage and 12a (5ha) of land, three cottages, three tofts and an additional 12 strips in the open fields. Thus the rector's manor mirrored the bishop's manor on a smaller scale.

The Corpus Christi archives also throw light on how the rector's manor was organised. In 1397 he employed a steward, bailiff, auditor, three carters, swineherd, shepherd, dairymaid, hayward (to look after hedges and fences) and a clerk to take the church services. They must have been instantly recognisable going about their business in the village for the bailiff was dressed in blue, the chaplain in green and the rest of the servants in striped red and green.

To run his estate successfully the rector needed a significant number of different buildings clustered around the rectory. In 1396 these were listed as the great barn, a stable, a sheepcote, a byre, two pigsties, a building for sifting flour, a bakehouse, a brewhouse and a coal house (for storing charcoal). In addition there was a garden for growing vegetables, nettles, hemp or cannabis (at least for fibres), plus a vineyard and orchard, and three fishponds on the line of Station Road. In 1396 Laurence the Welshman was paid £1.3s.4d. (£1.33p) to clean out the two small ponds on the side of the great pond. The water course shown on the Tithe map reaching down to The Old Farm probably evidences the last vestiges of the fishponds. All is now lost apart, perhaps, from the barn which might just be the origin of 23 and 25 Station Road. We can also gain some understanding from the records about the rectory itself. In 1397 it had a central hall with walls whitened with lime. The hall had an oriel window which needed mending in that year. Until about this time it appears the hall was open to the roof for the same record tells us a fireplace and chimney were being built in the great chamber, or main bedroom, which would have been at one end of the hall on an upper floor. It is difficult to know whether the rectory was built of stone or timber but the recording of a detached kitchen suggests a timber building at this time, so that if it caught fire the house itself would not have burned down. Also outside could be found the latrines. Whether it was already constructed of stone or whether it was later constructed of stone we will probably never know. Does the reference in these accounts to 33 cartloads of freestone from Cleeve Hill give us any clue? Although a survey of 1589 recorded 'a slated dwelling house' it could have been either timber or stone built. We know that after Timothy Gates moved from here to the former bishop's manor house, forty years later in 1665

This sketch of c.1700 shows The Priory in an earlier form, but without a door on the side facing the church

the building was described as dilapidated. What then happened is a bit of a puzzle. Today the front aspect is of a largely 18th-century mansion, but there are clues of an earlier state which might just contain elements of an earlier house, especially the large ashlar stone footings to the left of the doorway. The sketch of *c.*1700 shows an earlier arrangement of the windows, narrower gables and lacks a door. The western wall still has the drip moulds above the windows which are shown in the sketch and these were fashionable in this area in the late 17th and early 18th centuries. Only the blind window in the central gable remained when the sash windows were installed probably in the early 19th century. The Priory has never had the symmetry expected from a house built in one building campaign and in that perhaps lies clues to its links to the original rectory.

The western face of The Priory retains the earlier windows which were replaced on the front. A photograph taken in 1976

The Corpus Christi archive gives us a glimpse of the rectors' affluent lifestyle in the Later Middle Ages. Although the rectory garden had its own vines, in 1392-93 the rector, probably John de Brian, paid 2d (1p) to the almoner of Tewkesbury Abbey, who distributed the abbey's alms to the poor, for delivering 120 gallons of wine in one consignment to the rectory. This had come from Gascony to Bristol and then along the River Severn. One wonders how long this lasted because it was by no means the only wine which was ordered by the rector. Many other goods came up or down the River Severn to either Gloucester or Tewkesbury to be transported to the village. Sheep came from Worcester, logs from Bewdley, tables from Bristol, fish from Evesham. In addition, beds and blankets came from London, dishes, stools and buckets from Chipping Campden and wax for candles from Gloucester. His needs were met from afar.

So who were the rectors of Bishop's Cleeve during the Later Middle Ages? It is impossible to consider all of them, but a constant theme runs through the appointments and continued even until the start of the 20th century - the rectory provided a rich living to men who were already wealthy and often used to reward public servants who had no real intention of ever visiting Bishop's Cleeve. Some of these were of sufficient national significance that their entries can be found in the *Dictionary of National Biography*. For example Nicholas Bubwith (1406-1415) was appointed rector the day after he had been appointed Bishop of London and Lord Privy Seal by Henry IV. He then became Lord High Treasurer of England in 1407 and in the same year also Bishop of Bath and Wells, after brief spells as the Bishop of London and Bishop of Salisbury. We know that during his time as Bishop of Bath and Wells he never visited Bishop's Cleeve. You can read about Walter Scammell, who was rector from 1273-87, in the tour around St Michael's.

John Claymond was rector from 1517 to 1537. He was a national, even an international, scholar of the Renaissance who wrote a twenty volume commentary on the Roman writer and philosopher Pliny's work *Natural History* which itself contained thirty volumes and is still considered the first encyclopedia ever written. Claymond was also a friend of the great European Renaissance scholar Erasmus. So how did he come to be the rector of Bishop's Cleeve? In 1507 he became president of Magdalen College Oxford and then ten years later he was offered, and accepted, the presidency of a brand new college, Corpus Christi, which

The style of the dress suggests the rector's seal was in use at the time of Claymond and Parkhurst

was established to promote the new learning of the Renaissance. However, this meant a drop in income and so he was granted the rectory to compensate him. Although he was an international figure of great learning, he must have visited the village. John Basse, the parish priest, complained in an undated letter that he was not receiving his fees for taking mass and was weary as he had no-one to help him. The 'farmer', the person leasing the rectory manor from Claymond and who lived in the house, "speaks fair words but his deeds utter otherwise; there will never be love and charity among the parishioners while he continues as farmer". The letter ends with Basse promising to show Claymond the complaints against the farmer the next time he visited the village. Sadly we don't know the outcome of the case. Further evidence that Claymond took an interest in the village comes from his creating a scholarship in 1536 for a local boy at Brazenose College, which lasted three hundred years until 1857. It is most likely that it was through John Claymond that the records of the rectory came into the Corpus Christi archive.

Dr John Parkhurst

Another nationally significant figure who served as the rector in the 16th century was Dr John Parkhurst (rector 1548-54 and 1560-63). He was also an eminent Oxford scholar who wrote extensively and who turned the rectory into a centre for discussing Protestant ideas with his Oxford contemporaries. In 1543 he had been appointed chaplain to Queen Catherine Parr, who after the death of King Henry VIII married Sir Thomas Seymour and came to live at nearby Sudeley in 1547. When Catholic Queen Mary came to the throne in 1554 he fled abroad for safety, returning after Queen Elizabeth I succeeded her half sister in 1558. "Parkhurst has now gone to his people in Cleeve where he reigns like a king and looks down on bishops," wrote one of his reforming colleagues. In Bishop Hooper's survey of the diocese of Gloucester in 1552 it was recorded 'Mr John Parkhurst, rector, found very learned'. His curate 'Sir' Symon Baker could recite the Ten Commandments and knew that the Lord's prayer came from Matthew's gospel chapter eleven. This must have re-assured the bishop of the competence of the village clergy because in the 311 parishes of the diocese, only a quarter of the priests were described as 'fully competent' and ten could not even recite the Lord's Prayer! In 1560 John Parkhurst became Bishop of Norwich, but he did not relinquish the rectory until 1563. Compare his interest in the village with his successor, Richard Reeve, Queen Elizabeth I's chaplain, who was removed after only one year because the villagers complained that he had not appointed a priest to serve them and he showed no intention of moving to the village, which meant that they were without spiritual aid.

We now enter a more complicated episode in the history of the rectory - the move to the former bishop's manor house. As stated above, since at least 1418 part, if not all, of the rectory manor had been rented out so the rector could enjoy the income from it without the bother of administering it. In practice the rector did not have to be a clergyman. In March 1559 Thomas Cocks of Crowle in Worcestershire began to rent it for £84 (approximately £45,000 today) a year. Thomas was the clerk to the kitchen of the bishop and he leased the rectory from Seth Holland, the Dean of Worcester, who had succeeded John Parkhurst. There might have been some nepotism as Thomas married Seth Holland's extremely rich niece, which gave him the means to acquire substantial property in Worcestershire. It appears Thomas continued to rent the rectory lands when John Parkhurst returned to Bishop's Cleeve even though the latter instigated a court case against Seth Holland who he claimed had unlawfully usurped the rectory during his exile. The result of the case is not known but it can have made no difference to the lease. Perhaps it stalled when John Parkhurst became Bishop of Norwich or when Seth Holland died in 1561, leaving £700 (approximately £330,000 today) in his will. Unfortunately we don't know when Thomas actually bought the rectory with its land but he moved into the house with his wife Elizabeth and their four children in 1565; another twelve children were born in Bishop's Cleeve. There has been some debate whether they moved into the old rectory or the former bishop's manor house, however it is now quite clear they moved into the old rectory. In a survey of 1589 describing the land use around the rectory building there is a reference to the fishponds. These must have been the three which ran along what is now Station Road.

In 1587 Thomas acquired the right to choose the rector of Bishop's Cleeve and in 1592 he appointed one of his sons Peter to be 'preacher'. It is possible Peter became rector in his own right in 1594 but much more likely in 1603 after his father had died in 1601. At that time the rectory was worth £600 a year when the daily wage for a craftsman was 12d (5p), for an agricultural labourer 8d (3½p) and for servants even less, although these were provided with board and lodging. In 1607 Peter married Catherine Bridges, granddaughter of the first Lord Chandos of Sudeley, thus acquiring his wife's wealth and when Peter died young in 1612, aged 45, his successor as rector, Timothy Gates, married Catherine his widow. As all Peter's wealth had been left to his wife this must have been a major factor which enabled Timothy to purchase the former bishop's manor for £3000 (approximately £770,000 today) and live in the bishop's manor house from 1624. In 1665 the original rectory was described as dilapidated and, as discussed above, The Priory's architectural features suggest it was extensively renovated or completely rebuilt around that time. And there our jigsaw pieces for the moment mostly run out. However, we do know that it wasn't totally abandoned by the church. We find in the 1861 census that William Ellison the senior curate was living there with his wife and two children and a 16-year-old domestic servant. In 1881 he was still living there with his wife, daughter and a 17-year-old domestic servant. In 1861 the house was known as Priory House. This is the first recording I have found of the name, but that name has misled people into thinking monks lived here when St Michael's was once a monastery. This was never the case, as explained elsewhere.

By 1861 The Priory had just become a prestigious large house near the centre of the village. In 1839 the Tithe map shows that it stood in its own grounds and that the former stables had been converted into a house. From at least 1839 until his death shortly before the Enclosure Award of 1847 it was owned and lived in by John Morris who owned extensive property in the village, the rents of which provided him with an income. His property extended to 85 acres (35ha) with nine other houses and cottages. We don't know for how long after 1881 William

Ellison continued to live in The Priory but in 1901 Elizabeth Soll, an 85 year old widow of independent means was living there with a lady's maid, parlour maid and housemaid. Ten years later another widow, Henrietta Staunton (77) lived there with her 47 year old unmarried daughter Gertrude and a cook, housemaid and parlour maid. The two sick nurses also living there suggests Henrietta and Gertrude were not in the best of health. At this time the house was owned by a Mrs Parsons who lived in Charlton Kings. In 1919 Edward Franks, who was already living there, bought the house for £1850 (approximately £100,000 today!). His wife Ada had an interesting if tragic story to tell.

Ada was born in London in 1865, the daughter of Colonel Newman Burfoot Thoyts, an officer in the Indian army who retired to live in Pittville Circus Road in Cheltenham in 1876. Before he died in 1918 he had been mayor of the town three times. Before she was twenty five Ada had married Edward Eagar, a captain in the 5th Northumberland Fusiliers, and they had four sons. The marriage lasted barely ten years before the first tragedy hit Ada as her husband was killed fighting at the relief of Kimberley during the Boer War. Ada was not short of money as all four sons attended Sherborne public school in Dorset from where their third son Francis served as head boy before leaving in December 1912 to join the Woolwich Military Academy in February 1913 to follow in his late father's footsteps into the army. At the outbreak of the First World War in August 1914 he took up a commission as Lieutenant in the Royal Field Artillery. His war did not last long for he was killed at Fleurbaix in northern France in the following May, aged twenty one. He is commemorated on the village's war memorial and his gravestone stands in the church's graveyard with the inscription 'Until the day breaks and the shadows flee away' - words of a grieving mother.

Denis was still at Sherborne school when he learnt of his brother's

Francis Eagar (Sherborne School)

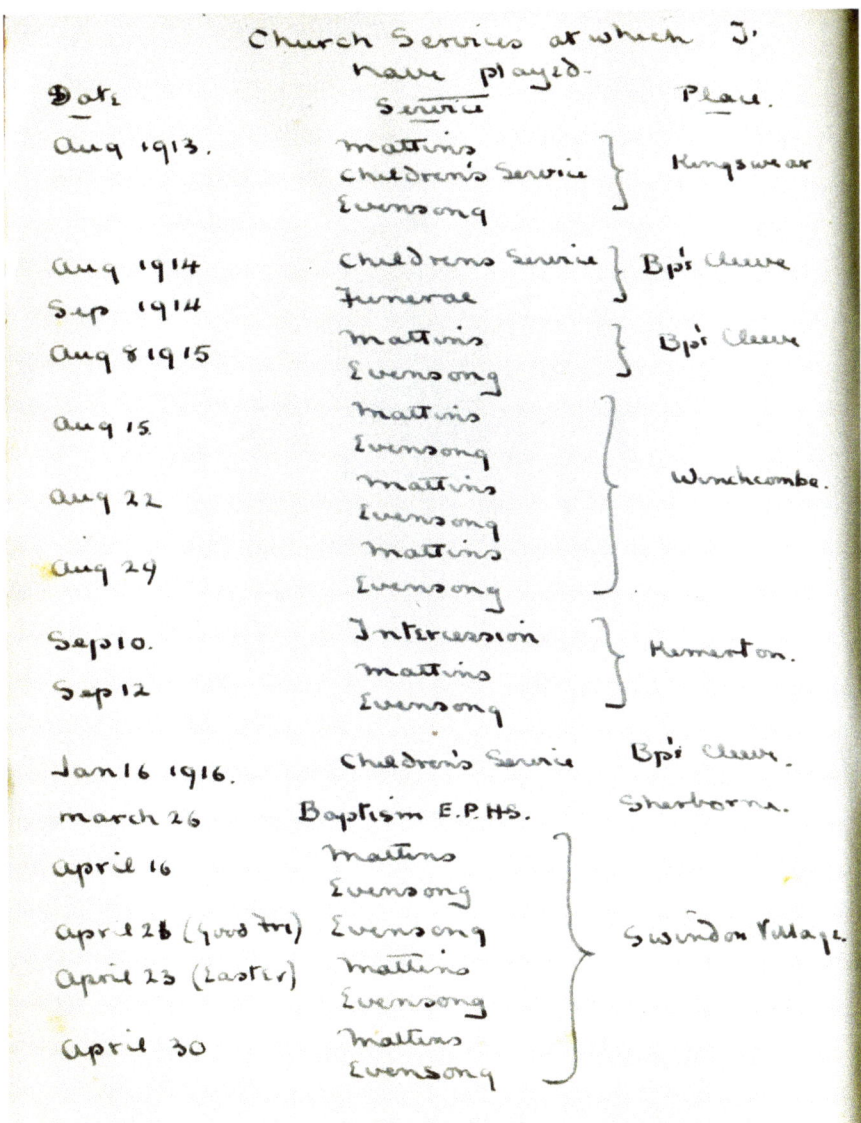

Denis's diary of playing the organ in local churches. He first played in St Michael's when he was just fifteen years old (Sherborne School)

death. He was the youngest son and unlike his older brothers had no intention of joining the army. He was a keen musician and at an early age an accomplished church organist who also wrote his own music. He was hoping to become ordained as a clergyman. He, too, served the school

Denis Eagar (Sherborne School)

well and secured a place at Keble College Oxford but was called up immediately he left school in 1917. Like Francis he served as a Lieutenant in the Royal Field Artillery. He was killed by a sniper on the edge of Wytschaete Wood in Flanders, Belgium in September 1918 barely six weeks before the end of the war. His commemoration is as one of the 34,991 names on the Tyne Cot memorial and his name is next to Francis on the war memorial. Ada heard of the death of her two sons whilst living at The Priory. Their deaths must have made her two surviving sons, who went on to live full lives, seem even more special.

Such are the stories behind the names on the village's war memorial, of lives cut short and talents never fulfilled. The war itself had little impact on village life, unlike the Second World War, but its real impact was felt by grieving families, such as the Franks at The Priory. Ada lived until 1951 and at times seems to have vied with Louisa Lascelles for the accolade of lady of the manor. On her death the house and its grounds were sold for £7500 (approximately £240,000 today). The Priory has continued to be the private residence of its owners.

CASE STUDY 5
THE OLD MANOR HOUSE

In 1561 the Bishop of Worcester's manor passed to Queen Elizabeth I. She soon granted it out and it then descended through a number of absentee owners until bought by Timothy Gates, rector of Bishop's Cleeve, in 1624. He bought it from Giles Broadway of Postlip for £3000 (approximately £¾m today), which included all the buildings and the land which extended to 486a (203ha). Giles had bought it himself only in 1618, for £2700. Thus the former bishop's manor house became the rectory and his barn became the Tithe Barn. Thirty five years later Timothy sold the land attached to the manor, keeping only the rectory

with its grounds and associated buildings. So what happened to the land attached to the bishop's manor?

There is a gap in the records until 1712 when we find that the manor was basically just a large farm. However the name 'manor house' had already been transferred from the former bishop's manor house. It passed through a succession of absentee owners but we know that in 1730 it was occupied by widow Fowler and her sons. In 1735 William Strahan, a London lawyer, bought the farm for £2930 (approximately £640,000 today). It was described as being 173a (72ha) in extent with rights of common pasture, mostly on Cleeve Hill where it also possessed the rights to quarry the sand and stone. This provided William with an annual rental income of £27. William bought it to add to the Haymes estate on the hill slope between Woodmancote and Southam, which he had acquired by marriage in 1707. He obviously fancied himself becoming the lord of the manor; in 1746 he built a family pew in the centre of the nave of St Michael's church.

Part of a cruck in the earlier part of the house

More importantly the design of The Old Manor House suggests William decided to impress the villagers by re-building the property into what we see today. Its predecessor, the house lived in by widow Fowler and her sons, was cruck-built and stood at right angles to the road and partly survives as a wing of the new house, being clad in the same Cleeve Hill stone from which the new house was constructed. William built it somewhat on the cheap. Expensive ashlar (cut) stone is confined to the corners and the walls are of smaller, rougher stone. This was then covered with stucco which was then grooved to look like ashlar. Nevertheless, in 1775 it was described as 'a good farmhouse of stone

The ashlar quoins show the chisel marks for the better adhesion of the stucco

and slate'. Despite this, William had no desire to leave Haymes and so his influence on the village was minimal. He died in 1773 and both manors were sold to two Worcester gentleman, John Thorneloe and William Lily for £7000 (approximately £1.1m today). Thorneloe then bought out Lilly for £3783. The manor house in Bishop's Cleeve at that time was tenanted by Richard Webb for an annual rental of £66.10s. (£66.50p). Thorneloe continued the custom that the owners were all absentees. By 1797 any manorial courts still held took place at Haymes.

We know that in 1812 John Minett was the tenant farmer. In 1839 it was owned by a Mrs Margaret Smith of Marylebone in London and farmed by William Roberts by which time its land had shrunk to 78a (31ha). By 1901 it had ceased to be a farm for in the census of that year the Manor House, as it was then called, was the home of Phoebe Lewis and her two daughters. Phoebe was 66 and living off a private income but by 1914 she had moved out and rented it to a Mrs Cartwright. She sold it in 1919 by which time it was being called The Old Manor House. In October 1937 it was sold to Frances Yerburgh, the widow of the Reverend William Werburgh, the rector of Bredon, who had died suddenly at the age of fifty five playing golf in June. Tragically two years later his widow took her own life.

It has continued as a family home to this day although in the 1950s some of its rooms were used as classrooms as the primary school along School Road expanded more quickly than classrooms could be added as Smiths estate grew. Today its former use as a farm can still be recognised from the timber-framed barn behind it, used as a garden room in 1951 but now converted to a dwelling, which can just be seen from Station Road.

CASE STUDY 6
EVERSFIELD HOUSE

IF THE WALLS of Eversfield House could speak what an interesting story they could tell! If the house looks untidy this is because it is the back; its front suggests it was built about the same time as The Priory. From the appearance of the building, you would never guess that Eversfield was a popular tourist attraction in the first half of the last century, putting Bishop's Cleeve firmly on the map.

Eversfield House in 1979 with the white bakery building to the left

In 1898 Andrew Denley bought the house with its bakery and a large orchard. With ever an eye to business he opened up the orchard as a tea and pleasure ground with secondhand attractions purchased from Charlton Kings. Closing down in the Great War he re-opened in 1919 with a flourish. His advertisement tells all about his intentions: 'Sunday Schools, Temperance Societies, Young People's Guilds, Mothers Unions etc, gladly take advantage of the unique facilities for spending an enjoyable outing. The grounds are situated just a few minutes walk from the Great Western Railway station, 3 miles north of Cheltenham but quite in the country.' In 1922 a large hall was built to the right of the house as a tea room to extend the accommodation. This also served as a village hall in the winter, which provided an income when the pleasure grounds were closed.

Eversfield's bakery delivery van advertised the Tea Gardens

The grounds were open each year from Easter Monday to mid-September, but never on Sunday. The crowds poured in from as far away as Worcester and Stratford, the Forest of Dean and Chipping Norton and Chipping Sodbury. Large parties such as St Paul's Sunday School in Cheltenham hired a train, although by the 1930s increasing numbers came in charabancs. These caused parking problems in Station Road until Alick Denley, Andrew's son, created a car park on the east side of Eversfield House. Visitors could just sit and enjoy ice cream and other refreshments, enjoying a good plain tea at 9d (3½p) or a cheaper tea for 6d (2½p) promised by the slogan 'A Square Deal and a Square Meal'. They could watch a show or play tennis, but most came to experience the varied attractions. To our eyes they seem primitive and they were nearly all made of wood and hand operated – a miniature big wheel, swings, seesaw, slides, helter-skelter, coconut shies, a cart with an axle off-set on its two wheels and railways which were hand operated with a small car being pushed up a wooden ramp and allowed to run down it. The slide had to be treated with paraffin to avoid splinters; health and safety precautions were totally absent! In the 1930s a stage was erected for performances. Teams were provided by an army of lady helpers and visitors could buy souvenir mugs and rock imprinted with 'A Present from Bishop's Cleeve'.

The amusements stretched back to Priory Lane. Note the self-propelled 'railway' on the right of the photograph

The outbreak of the war in 1939 led to the closure of the tea and pleasure grounds and at different times during the war its tearooms became billets used by the army and air force, and lodgings for evacuated schoolchildren. In January 1940 all the evacuee children from Birmingham were treated to tea. In May 1945 ninety village children celebrated victory in the war by being entertained to tea, but the pleasure grounds never re-opened. The attractions themselves had deteriorated for lack of maintenance and now appeared decidedly old-fashioned. In April 1946 all the attractions and catering equipment were sold off. However, the bakery attached to the main house continued until 1986. The former tea room continued to serve for a few years as a village hall but *c.*1958 it was sold and then used for industrial purposes until it was demolished in 1987 and houses built on its site. Houses were already being built on the pleasure ground itself, and so all traces of Eversfield Tea and Pleasure Grounds were removed. They were confined to history. For more details of their story, see David Denley's *Eversfield Tea and Pleasure Grounds*. See *Further Reading* for the details.

GLOSSARY

acre an area of land approximately half the size of a football pitch (abbreviated to 'a')
aisle a part of a church divided from the nave by a row of columns
bailiff the lord's estate manager
beadle an official with several responsibilities for the lord, e.g. carrying messages, ensuring tenants came to the manor court
chancel the part of a church near the altar, traditionally reserved for the clergy and choir
cotlander in Bishop's Cleeve a medieval tenant holding about 6 acres who carried out labour services
croft a small pice of enclosed agricultural land often within the village
curate an assistant to the rector and paid by him; also called a **clerk**
demesne land retained by the lord for his own use cultivated for him by his tenants but in the Later Middle Ages increasingly rented out. The produce was for the use of the landholder and his officials and also sold for profit
enclosure the process carried out by an act of parliament by which the land of the open fields was converted into smaller fields with boundaries, also called enclosures
estate historically all the manors of one landowner formed an estate; sometimes used synonymously with manor. In modern times the term is usually used to define a housing development
glebe land held by the parish church
hectare an area of land approximately 2.4 acres in size (abbreviated to 'ha')
hall the main room in a medieval house and open to the roof
labour service the work a tenant was expected to carry out on the lord's demesne as part of the rent; this declined in the Later Middle Ages as tenants increasingly paid in money
mondayman in Bishop's Cleeve a medieval tenant holding about 3 acres owing a labour service on Mondays
manor an area of land over which the lord had control; also the house

where the lord lived
messuage a house or farm with associated buildings on a small plot of land
nave the central part of a church
open field farmland divided into strips which were divided among the tenants without fences or hedges and subjected to agreed routines for growing and harvesting crops and leaving fallow (uncultivated)
plough a measurement of land in Domesday Book generally agreed to refer to a team of eight oxen which could plough about 100 acres each year
rector the person entitled to receive all the tithes from a parish
rectory all the land and property belonging to a rector; also the house where the rector lived
reeve one tenant chosen by the other tenants to organise the daily business of the manor and represent them before the lord
Reformation the changes in the church started by Henry VIII in the sixteenth century which meant the church in England and Wales broke away from the Roman Catholic church and became known as a Protestant church
Renaissance refers to a period in European civilization which was marked by a revival of Classical (i.e. Greek and Roman) learning and wisdom.
ridge and furrow the corrugated pattern seen in fields which was created by the method of medieval ploughing when the first furrow was opened in the centre and the plough worked outwards parallel to the first furrow
tithe a tenth of all the produce from the land given annually to the rector; converted to money payments by an act of parliament in 1836 and abolished exactly a century later
toft a plot of land where a building did stand but now empty
transept the two parts of a church forming the arms of the cross shape
vestry an unelected body of the main landowners which governed the village before being replaced by elected parish councillors in 1894
yardlander in Bishop's Cleeve a medieval tenant holding about 24 acres who carried out labour services

FURTHER READING

D.H. Aldred, *A History of Bishop's Cleeve and Woodmancote* (Stroud, 2009)
D. Aldred and T. Curr, *In and Around Bishop's Cleeve through Time* (Stroud, 2009)
D. Aldred and T. Curr, *In and Around Bishop's Cleeve through Time: A Second Selection* (Stroud, 2010)
D. Charnock, *Oldacre: A Gloucestershire Family and Business 1881-1986* (Lewes, 1990)
D. Denley, *Eversfield Tea and Pleasure Grounds Bishop's Cleeve* (Falmouth, 1997)
C. Dyer, *Lords and Peasants in a Changing Society* (Cambridge, 1980)
C. Ellis (ed.), *Smiths Industries at Cheltenham* (Surbiton, 1990)
C. Elrington (ed.), *The Victoria History of the County of Gloucester, Volume VIII* (London, 1968)
E. Powell, *Parish Church of St Michael and All Angels, Bishop's Cleeve* (Privately published, no date)

The following useful websites were accessible at the time of writing:
Gloucestershire Archives catalogue - https://www.gloucestershire.gov.uk/archives/online-catalogue/ (Search 'Bishop's Cleeve')
Images of Bishop's Cleeve - https://www.imagesofbishopscleeve.info/
Know Your Place - https://maps.bristol.gov.uk/kyp/?edition=glos (Search 'Bishop's Cleeve')
Lloyd George Survey of Land Values: Gloucestershire - https://www.glos1909survey.org.uk/index.html (Search 'Bishop's Cleeve')
National Library of Scotland historic Ordnance Survey maps - https://maps.nls.uk/os/6inch-england-and-wales/index.html (Search 'Bishop's Cleeve')
Transactions of the Bristol and Gloucestershire Archaeological Society - https://www.bgas.org.uk/publications/transactions-main-page (Search 'Bishop's Cleeve')
Conversion of historic money values to modern values from: https://www.statista.com/statistics/1031884/value-pound-sterling-since/

www.ingramcontent.com/pod-product-compliance
Lightning Source LLC
Chambersburg PA
CBHW041927090426
42743CB00021B/3468